REIMAGINING WORK

Strategies

to Disrupt Talent,

Lead Change, and Win

with a Flexible Workforce

ROB BIEDERMAN

PAT PETITTI

PETER MAGLATHLIN

WILEY

Published by John Wiley & Sons, Inc., Hoboken, New Jersey.
Published simultaneously in Canada

For general information about our other products and services, please contact our Customer Care Department within the United States at (800) 762-2974, outside the United States at (317) 572-3993 or fax (317) 572-4002.

Wiley publishes in a variety of print and electronic formats and by print-on-demand. Some material included with standard print versions of this book may not be included in e-books or in print-on-demand. If this book refers to media such as a CD or DVD that is not included in the version you purchased, you may download this material at http://booksupport.wiley.com. For more information about Wiley products, visit www.wiley.com.

Library of Congress Cataloging-in-Publication Data is available:

ISBN 978-1-119-38956-9 (Hardcover)
ISBN 978-1-119-38968-2 (ePDF)
ISBN 978-1-119-38965-1 (ePub)

Cover Design: Wiley
Cover Image: © FatCamera / Getty Images

Printed in the United States of America

10 9 8 7 6 5 4 3 2 1

From Rob

Three key groups have been indispensable to HourlyNerd/Catalant's success. To our incredible team, who has bet precious unrecoverable time chasing this dream with us, thank you. To our investors, for your irrational faith in us and in the idea, we are eternally grateful. And, to our experts and customers, who share our audacious belief in a future of work that allows people to live life by their own design, we are honored to be on this journey with you.

Mom, Dad, and Brooke: each of you inspire me every day.

For all of the founders who've had doors slammed in their faces and been told by experts their ideas would never work: never, ever, ever, ever, ever give up.

From Pat

Starting a company is really, really hard and can't be done without an exceptionally supportive family willing to let you chase your dreams working long hours in the face of likely failure, incredible, dedicated and inspiring cofounders who push you to be your very best and pull you through the hard times, an amazing team that believes and perseveres when everything tells them not to, investors who give you the support to think big, make mistakes, and take bold risks, and users who push you to continually improve while understanding why things aren't always perfect.

We have been so fortunate to have all of the above and more, and for that I am eternally grateful.

From Peter

I'd like to thank my mother and father, Laurie and Peter Maglathlin, my two sisters, Caroline and Phoebe Maglathlin, and my fiancee, Caitlin O'Malley, for their unwavering support and encouragement. I'd also like to thank the faculty, students, and alumni of Harvard Business School for providing us the opportunity and the platform to make our dream a reality. Lastly, I'd like to thank our investors for believing in our vision when few others did, and for partnering with us on this journey.

Contents

About Us

Catalant connects companies to the world's best business talent, on demand. We believe that rapid advances in technology and remarkable changes in how professionals today are choosing to work has transformed the way companies and talent engage with each other. At Catalant, we have built a platform for these seekers and suppliers of talent to meet. Our global network includes 40,000+ independent professionals and subject matter experts who are available to work with enterprise customers on a range of business needs including research, strategy, marketing, finance, sales, and operations projects. There is a new way of working and Catalant is helping to drive the change. Based in Boston, Catalant serves hundreds of global clients, including more than 25% of the Fortune 100. For more information, visit www.GoCatalant.com

About the Authors

ROB BIEDERMAN

Rob Biederman is the cofounder and co-CEO of Catalant, where he is responsible for sales and key enterprise relationships, marketing, global partnerships and finance in addition to shared governance of the company.

Prior to founding Catalant, Biederman was a private equity investor at Goldman Sachs and Bain Capital, where he focused on the health care and high-tech industries. Biederman graduated from Princeton University and Harvard Business School.

PATRICK PETITTI

Patrick Petitti is the cofounder and co-CEO of Catalant and is responsible for the technology and product development, software enterprise relationships, HR and shared governance for the company.

Prior to founding Catalant, Petitti was a consultant at negotiation and conflict management consulting firm Vantage partners, and before that at Booz Allen Hamilton. Petitti received his BS from the Massachusetts Institute of Technology and MBA from the Harvard Business School. He is a born-and-raised Bostonian.

PETER MAGATHLIN

Peter Maglathlin is the cofounder and former CFO of Catalant Technologies.

Prior to founding Catalant Technologies, Peter worked at UBS Investment Bank in the Financial Institutions Group and Highbridge Capital Management in Corporate Development. Peter is also actively involved in the Big Brother Big Sister Organization of Massachusetts Bay. Originally from Connecticut, Peter is a graduate of Harvard College and Harvard Business School.

Right people, right place, right time. Working with partners, not always permanent employees.

—A respondent at a Future of Work conference when asked, "What does the Future of Work Mean to You?"

Introduction

We're sure there have been worse presentations in the history of business. But our first effort to sell the idea for the company we now call Catalant was memorably weak.

It was the winter of 2013, and we were halfway through our first year at Harvard Business School. HBS, as it is known in the vernacular, had only recently created a mandatory class aimed at giving every MBA student a taste of start-up life. That January, the entire first-year class of 900 broke into teams of six. The assignment: come up with a real-life business idea and then spend the next few months proving its viability. The first big test came a few days into the semester, when each team had to pitch its idea to their fellow students, who would then bid up or down shares of the company listed on a mock stock market. It was akin to a classroom version of the hit show *Shark Tank*. We learned the hard way that becoming a start-up rock star at HBS could be just as brutal as the television version.

Back then, we were calling our fledgling company Rent-A-Nerd. The concept was relatively simple. Small, entrepreneurial, mostly owner-run businesses needed help with issues like marketing and strategy, same as their larger counterparts. These well-known corporate behemoths were well accustomed to turning to the stalwart, blue-chip business of management consulting for their solutions. However, the smaller companies we were targeting couldn't afford the services of a big consulting firm like McKinsey or Bain. One of us had already worked at a large consulting firm prior to arriving at HBS. So had many of our classmates. Big company consulting was the lingua franca at HBS. That's where our concept took flight. What if we challenged these rulers of the universe and disrupted the traditional model? What if there was a way to help small business owners and in the same breath, turn old-school consulting upside down on its head?

At the time we hatched our idea, we were suggesting the equivalent of a Craigslist website for small businesses and MBAs. Our company would be a matchmaking service that allowed small businesses to enlist, at an affordable price, the services of MBA students from the country's top business schools, to share their expertise. And just in case that database was not quite seasoned enough, what if we threw in the weight of the top schools' alumni as well? We proposed to "match" small businesses to a talent pool of tried and proven experts. The small business could post a project on our platform, and anyone enrolled at a top-tier business school with an email address to prove it could bid on the job. What was our equation for success? The small business solves their work problem. The hungry grad student gets a paycheck, not to mention some very nice CV padding. And our fledgling company would take its cut as a percentage of completed deals, thus generating a revenue stream. On the surface, it made perfect sense to us. Why not put it out there?

There were 900 students in our first-year class. The school divided us into 10 sections of 90 each. The 15 teams in our section, Section F, pitched the "investors" of Section J, who then would trade shares in our 15 companies on the simulated stock market. The stocks of the start-ups that seemed most promising would rise, while the prices of those that seemed most far-fetched would fall. This would be the first benchmark in a competition that lasted through the spring. The true winner would presumably be the company that won in this simulated marketplace.

Everyone sharpened their tools and dug in. It soon became apparent that our competition, the 14 other groups of Section F, had sharper pencils than we did. They were creating these incredible multimedia presentations. You'd think they'd all just walked out of the latest Microsoft PowerPoint refresher course with a gold star. No bells and whistles were too much. In contrast, we had thrown together maybe a half dozen slides, including one of Scrooge McDuck (yes, Donald Duck's uncle!) jumping into a pile of coins. We had wanted to reinforce the moneymaking aspect of our endeavor, but the sight gag fell as flat as day-old coffee.

As Idea Pitch Day fast approached, our problems multiplied when one-third of our brain trust, Pat, tragically lost a cousin just before our presentation. So now we were one man down with a Disney cartoon character as our ace in the hole, positioned against a roster of future wannabe TED presenters. It wasn't until late the night before Pitch Day that we even figured out who was going to say what. Suffice it to say, things were looking grim.

Come the Big Day, we sat in stony silence, watching as one Fortune 500–worthy pitch after another rolled off the tongues and laptops of our competitors. When our turn finally arrived, we took the stage and let it rip. We came off disjointed and ill prepared, not to mention the fact that our presentation was considerably shorter than the others. Our fellow judges—the faux potential investors—peppered us with questions, exposing our lack of preparation. Apparently, the future investors of Section J were thick with students who had worked for large management consulting firms prior to business school. They were dubious of our prospects, to say the least. The big firms, we were unceremoniously informed, had a "secret sauce" that our business start-up could never replicate. And the smaller boutique firms offered access to a caliber of specialist we could never attract to our platform. One woman even stood to say that her group had thought of our very idea themselves, but they had actually done some market research and rejected it hands down after concluding that small businesses weren't interested. "What makes you think *you're* going to succeed?" she asked in an incredulous voice. We took turns looking at one another and intermittently inspecting the shoes on our feet. We didn't have a clue.

Once we had finished suffering through the 14 other meticulously prepared pitches, the school's simulated stock market opened for business. By day's end shares in our company were trading dead last—150th of the 150 companies launched that day. *Nice job!*

We were back in our room licking our wounds when an email popped in from our section professor. Kudos was not the order of the day. "You phoned it in," he began. The presentation was flat, the support materials sketchy. Even *we* didn't seem excited by the idea, he cajoled. Adding insult to injury, he brought up the holes in our pitch that our fellow students were able to poke entire fists through. "If you still intend to pursue this as your business project, you need to pick it up," he warned. Our humiliation was complete.

Criticism is sometimes easy to slough off. Dismiss the source and with it the negative feedback presented. But these were our HBS peers and presumably some of the best and brightest young business minds in the country. And they were telling us that our idea was so bad they were valuing it at less than the six T-shirt companies that were pitched that day. We even lagged behind an app for free hugs.

We were embarrassed, as well we should have been. But we were also furious. We knew we were better than our subpar performance suggested. We also believed our idea was better than the lion's share of what we saw that day, and we were determined to prove it—to our classmates, but even more so to ourselves. We grabbed a screenshot of the class rankings to remember how horribly we had performed. Pat laid down the gauntlet for our team and vowed to tattoo the company logo on his backside if we could regroup and end the year in first place. He was challenging us to shame him for life on the backs of our success.

Rent-a-Nerd had been Rob's idea, and he seemed to take the rebuke from our classmates even more personally than the rest of us. "They're basically telling me I'm the stupidest person on campus," he said. Based on our stellar pitch and end of day one ratings, it was hard to argue with him.

But out of the ashes, something else was going on. This spirit of injustice, tempered with our fierce will to compete, was creating a spark of something in our room that night that refused to fizzle out. Looking back, honestly, if we had done a half-decent job of selling the company in the first place and ended up in the middle of the pack at the end of Pitch Day, there might not be the company we run today known as Catalant. There was something uniquely humiliating about our dead-last finish that fired up our competitive juices. We commiserated over our failure, wrote it off, and threw ourselves into the project of converting Rent-a-Nerd into a real business.

As the year unfolded, there would be more stumbles and more setbacks awaiting us. Still, the root of our idea felt like it was sprouting wings, and we had aspirations that far exceeded our classroom on the Charles. Emboldened, when the semester ended, we decided to take a flyer and travel to the West Coast to talk with potential investors. Between us, we were able to dust off enough connections to secure meetings with partners at nearly two dozen top-tier Silicon Valley venture firms. As awesome as that felt in the planning stages, the reality translated into a far gloomier tableau. Anyone who ever suggests that pitching to the Valley is sexy has not spent days listening to West Coast venture capitalists tell you how little they think of you and your idea. What's more, truth be told, we had not ventured all that far from our original less-than-impressive Pitch Day debut. Case in point, one morning we found ourselves sitting in the parking garage on Microsoft's Redmond campus, chugging coffee, pumping ourselves up to music, and counting down the minutes until we were ready to go in and shake things up. It's amazing we even heard the phone beep with a text. "Where the hell are you guys? We're all sitting here waiting for you!" It seemed we were well on our way to becoming an HBS case study in how *not* to start a business!

Still, we muscled—or muddled, as the case at times was—through our West Coast tour. The summer between our first and second year of graduate school began with days of rejections up and down Sand Hill Road. However, and most improbably, it ended with a big check from *Shark Tank* star and business maven Mark Cuban who, along with an angel investor named Bob Doris, gave us the seed money we needed to see if our idea of a marketplace for high-priced business talent might be a real business.

❖ ❖ ❖

"Careful what you wish for" should be taught on day one at every business school in America. We were still in our second year at HBS when we raised a Series "A" round of venture financing totaling in the millions. Despite the skepticism expressed by some of the visionaries who populate the Bay Area, three of stodgy Boston's best-regarded venture firms saw the potential of our fledgling company. Beyond our earliest and wildest expectations, there'd be a "B" round and then a "C" and then a "D" round that gave us a paper value in the hundreds of millions, much of that coming from New England. It was fortunate that we were die-hard fans of the Patriots, now that we were included in the roster of the Kraft family, who owns the fabled five-time Super Bowl–winning football team. Intuit founder Scott Cook, Rent the Runway founder Jenn Hyman, and several other tech luminaries also jumped onboard.

Luck was definitely smiling on us when we landed General Electric and its $140 billion in annual revenue as a true, paying customer. Going back to our drawing board days, a mere

18 months previous, we had initially thought we were creating a platform for small businesses. But bringing GE on board while we were still in grad school opened us up to a future that we had hardly imagined. General Electric proved more than a marquee customer. Its investment arm, GE Ventures, would take an ownership stake in our company and, more importantly, help champion our cause. Then-CEO Jeff Immelt, one of the business world's most highly regarded executives, would host a dinner in Boston on our behalf in the fall of 2016. Talk about executive buy-in! Jeff himself sent the invite emails to the CEOs of 15 of the country's largest companies, encouraging them to learn more about how our company could help them both manage costs and provide access to a wide array of top talent. Multiple senior leaders from the Fortune 100 showed up for our little dinner—a gathering that might have ranked among the more impressive turnouts of corporate firepower in Boston that year. Standing before the group, Jeff encouraged them to use Catalant and told them that our business had the potential to change the world. At the same time, a small part inside all of us recalled that screen grab of our 150th place finish, which Rob still regularly reviewed for motivation.

By 2017, more than 120 of the Fortune 1000 would be using Catalant to supplement their workforce, including GE, Staples, Medtronic, and IBM—to name just a few.

We can flatter ourselves and claim investors and corporate icons were drawn to Catalant because they saw something in the three of us. Perhaps. But we know the primary reason these influential movers and shakers became interested in our small company was our initial idea of creating a marketplace to find side work for MBA students and recent grads, wedded to the needs of a talent-starved corporate America. In fact, we still pinch ourselves that our classroom brainstorm has morphed into a platform that has the potential to upend the way businesses manage their talent.

We had only wanted to prove that our idea wasn't as lame as our fellow students thought. Instead, we had stumbled onto a new way for businesses of all sizes to get tasks done.

In 2015, Rob cowrote an article with Andrei Hagui, an associate professor in the strategy group at HBS, called "The Dawning of the Age of Flex Labor." It began, "The prevailing paradigm of people working as full-time employees for a single organization has outlived its usefulness." The point was that technology was fueling a seismic shift in work—and businesses that chose to ignore this did so at their own peril. The paper continued, "Our vision is straightforward: most people will become independent contractors who have the flexibility to work part-time for several organizations at the same time, or do a series of short, full-time gigs with different companies over the course of a year." What Rob and Professor Hagui were basically acknowledging was that despite our humble beginnings, we were offering a vision that threatened to disrupt the workplace.

We weren't surprised that those on the supply side—the workers—would see merit in a talent marketplace like we were building. The era of Dilbert and a workplace satirized by the comedic and the cubicle had been replaced by *Office Space*, with its maddening futility and fathomless promise of life married to an unfulfilling job. We weren't just grad students who had lucked out in the VC world. We were also employees who understood that we are fated to spend more time working than we do anything else, including sleep.[1] And with that knowledge, we were painfully aware that too many people are unhappy in their work. Polling shows that a majority of us find work a grind; as many as three in four feel disengaged and unfulfilled. Who wants to set off on that cruise?

---

[1] Jacob Morgan, *The Future of Work: Attract New Talent, Build Better Leaders, and Create a Competitive Organization* (Hoboken, NJ: John Wiley & Sons, 2014), xiii.

Our young business was building on the sociological capital that disaffection instinctually numbs us as millennials. The data show that this group—our colleagues—demand more of a work/life balance than previous generations. And if that means receiving 1099s each year from several places of work rather than a single W-2 from a single employer, so be it. We are the foot soldiers in a generation that insists on more flexibility at the workplace and less constrictive, more accommodating working relationships. A study by Deloitte, a giant of the consulting world (yes, we recognize the irony in quoting the likes of Deloitte), showed that three-quarters of millennials want the freedom to work remotely. Our generation is clamoring for a different relationship to work. Now that we represent one-third of the workforce and soon will represent the majority, it's quite possible we'll make it happen. As the founders of Catalant, we just happened to have the good fortune to unearth a missing piece of the equation: a platform that lets people work as free agents. Catalant has given the next generation access to a range of interesting, well-paying projects to keep them as busy as they need or want to be. Already more than 40,000 experts have found our marketplace, and it seems inevitable given the broader trend lines that eventually that number will swell to 400,000, if not 4 million—so long as we can provide them with a steady river of business that is accessible through the site.

The shock for us was on the demand side—that companies of all sizes were also clamoring for change. We found one study showing that 79 percent of large businesses felt they had an engagement problem with their workforce. And 85 percent, according to that same research, were struggling to retain top talent.[2] Since the 2008 Great Recession, corporations have been beggars in the war for talent, we learned from Joseph Fuller,

---

[2]Deloitte by Bersin, Global Human Capital Trends, 2014 (https://dupress .deloitte.com/dup-us-en/focus/human-capital-trends/2014.html).

a professor of management practices at HBS, who eventually would serve as a board observer for our company. And given the strategic advantage of a business remaining nimble, not to mention onboarding complexity and the like, businesses might logically choose to shift their mix of permanent employees and free agents. That was the conclusion of an Intuit report predicting that by 2020, "traditional employees will no longer be the norm, replaced by contingent workers such as freelancers and part-time workers." The rub, according to the literature, was how the more agile, forward-thinking businesses would find the talent once they had made this shift. More than one in five businesses (21 percent) identified "finding qualified freelancers" as the single biggest employment challenge, according to a study by Tower Lane.[3] Two-thirds (68 percent) expressed a "strong" or "very strong" interest in a tool that would enable easier and quicker hiring and onboarding of freelancers.

What we've learned in talking to Catalant customers is that even those at the top echelons of the country's better-known, big-brand name companies are feeling frustrated. Recruiting and employee retention are huge pain points for just about any corporation located outside of a New York or San Francisco. As lovely as Cincinnati, Peoria, or Moline might be, most of today's most coveted college graduates want to live in a short list of major urban centers. The action, it turns out, is a big draw.

We also heard our share of complaints about the inefficiency of the system under which large, unwieldy companies operated. Sometimes they felt as if they had too many people on staff. At other times it felt as if they didn't have enough. One executive, who oversaw a staff that numbered in the tens of thousands, told us he often felt he didn't have the right talent in-house to start

---

[3]A study via the platform? Tower Lane—if transcriber heard it right—seems a one-person operation, https://www.linkedin.com/company/tower-lane-consulting.

with. Maybe the biggest surprise in our on-the-job education was that even the seemingly powerful inside most U.S. corporations felt powerless. As a result, when faced with a challenge, they turned to a giant consulting firm because they often could see no other way. Yet for all those millions of dollars companies paid, the consultants rarely delivered the news management most needed to hear. There's an inefficiency baked into a company that can't grow or shrink as the product cycle demands, and add or subtract skills sets as they are needed.

Technology is doing its part to usher in a more decentralized workplace. We can videoconference via Skype, Google Hangouts, or Cisco WebEx. It's easy to share files using Google Docs, Dropbox, or Box—and for those who really are serious about online collaboration tools and networks, there are cool new products like Slack. There's also been a corresponding rise in co-working spaces that allow people to rent a desk by the hour, day, or month. That strikes us as some of the early infrastructure work needed to build out the free agent economy, much like gas stations were needed to create a car culture.

The last technological piece of the puzzle? Unicorn stars of the gig economy have brought marketplaces up to speed for people wanting to sell their services to consumers. But what about those who want to sell their services to businesses? Fortunately for us, this notion of a human cloud that allows any company to find any expert no matter what the task or project was gaining currency worldwide.

It's our view that much of what is said and written about the future of work seems overly narrow in focus. It's never more obvious than when one of us is asked to speak at a "Future of Work" conference. The field seems to have spawned its own cottage industry of soothsayers and experts eager to charge lots of money for their advice. Small, incremental steps to "transform your workplace" are the coin of the realm at these gatherings.

Workers seem desperate. So do their employers. Yet the solutions offered are mere Band-Aids: airier workspaces, or more flexible schedules to accommodate both early and late risers. The more innovative voices recommended doing away with a count on vacation days, or allowing employees to figure out for themselves what tools or systems they needed to work at peak efficiency. Still, when a company perceives a crisis in its culture or its numbers, it responds with a new version of casual Friday, or free bagels in the mornings and permission to telecommute every other Thursday. Not exactly the stuff of sea change.

We saw these issues rear their heads at a private gathering we held at our offices in the fall of 2016 for the HR directors of 15 of the country's most innovative businesses. We spent a day-and-a-half brainstorming ideas and hearing from experts in the field. Among the things we learned from such cutting-edge software and technology giants? Everyone seems to be feeling their way through the various crises and logjams. The good news is that the most successful businesses are open to thinking in a different way. They want to learn about the possibilities and opportunities of a project-based approach to work that gives them the flexibility to access the best people in a dynamic talent market.

But it goes further than that. What we're advocating for is nothing short of a complete disruption in the way businesses spend money on labor. A company needs permanent employees, of course, but technology allows for a radical shift in the mix of full-time and free agents. While one group may stay in-house and hold up the fort, there can still be a stable of regular go-to talent that is called in on a need-be basis. Think of it is as more of a Hollywood approach, where the talent is brought on board whenever a company needs the horsepower to take care of a given project. Companies will no doubt have their core of reliable stars. Just as a director tends to go back to the same cinematographer, a business would have its regular consultants whose invoices fluctuate quarter to quarter depending on the project load. These stars can hunker down as full-time employees because sometimes that just works better for people. But others may want to test the waters of the on-demand workplace.

Managers don't need to bear hug their employees and never let them go. What about giving them freedom, if that's what it takes to retain their occasional services and keep them both happy and working part-time for you? Maybe a person wants to travel less for the job because of kids, or conversely, just likes the challenge and stimulation of working on different kinds of projects each month. These on-demand pioneers would be free to say yes or no to a project depending on what else they had going on and what else they needed. For us, the goal should be giving both sides the flexibility to operate at peak efficiency. Businesses have access to talent when they need it—and people are able to do their best work every day.

Shouldn't that be the future of work?

CHAPTER 1

A Quick History of Work

The caveman was the original freelancer. He honed a skill, put it to work, and with any luck, made a subsistence living. There is not much record keeping on the numbers from back then, but the species persevered, so we can assume it was step one on the road to today's workplace.

At some point, trade and commerce began, perhaps in prehistoric times or maybe after that, depending on which historians you believe. Regardless, over the millennia a system evolved that allowed people to move their goods. Hunters could trade pelts for spices or teas and the bowls and utensils needed to eat. People learned about agriculture and created farms. A feudal system later emerged: serfs working on a lord's estate—in his fields, mines, and forests. Skilled trades developed: the blacksmith, the silk craftsman, the stonemason. A merchant class emerged. These were people fundamentally out for themselves in the developing marketplace—the small businessman or, to use today's terminology, the entrepreneur.

The seventeenth century saw the birth of the modern-day corporation—a legal construct that created a way for a group of people to act as a single entity. The Dutch East India Company was formed in 1602, and the Hudson's Bay Company, a Canadian entity, was incorporated a few decades later.

The first Industrial Revolution dates back to the mechanization of the textile industry in England in the late eighteenth century. That means that around the time the British were losing the Revolutionary War, they were also helping to revolutionize production.

Garments once painstakingly made by hand could now be stamped out by machines, powered by steam engines. Giant cotton mills sprung up around England, replacing weavers' cottages, and the factory was born. The early twentieth century welcomed the workingman wisdom of Henry Ford and saw the start of the second Industrial Revolution. This was the era of mass production and assembly lines: people performing the same basic task over and over again. By the 1950s, we minted the Organization Man, and then the Sixties rejected that, in part as a backlash against the dark side of being a cog in the corporate wheel. It was the birth of the individual creative spark in the workplace—the early stirrings of modern innovation—as we know it today.

Disruptive innovation, however, dates back at least to the weavers' cottages, if not before. There were no doubt some unhappy monks when Gutenberg's printing press made it unnecessary for them to copy all those books by hand. The cotton mills rendered the handloom largely obsolete, just as Ford would put a lot of carriage makers out of business with mass-produced cars. Yet the very tangible upside of progress was cleverly illustrated just a few years ago by a man named Andy George, who decided to make a chicken sandwich from scratch. George pickled his own cucumbers and made his own cheese. He harvested the wheat needed to make the bread and raised and killed a chicken for the meat. The preparation of this one sandwich took him six months and cost $1,500.[1] A darned-fine chicken salad aside, there's a lot to be said for division of labor, mechanization, and mass-market capitalism. Without it, we'd be so busy tending our cows and growing our vegetables that we wouldn't have time to search for a cure for cancer or new energy resources, much less catch up on our Netflix and Hulu series.

---

[1] Steven Hoffer, "Man Spends 6 Months, $1,500 to Make ONE Sandwich from Scratch," HuffPost, September 17, 2015, www.huffingtonpost.com/entry/1500-sandwich-from-scratch_us_55fabea1e4b08820d9177a2e.

The widespread, affordable personal computer has ushered in the third Industrial Revolution. The Internet and other digital technologies have upended and transformed entire industries. Nothing remains untouched. From the smallest player to the multinational behemoths, everything is monitored, tracked, and digitized. The ruthless quest for efficiency has helped mark this era. Technology has made possible on-demand manufacturing and just-in-time ordering. Artificial intelligence and virtual reality are moving us from the realm of the factory to the furthest excesses of the imagination. We're embracing driverless cars and three-dimensional printing, while drones are taking the place of factory workers and delivery drivers. Machine learning is stepping in where experts and judgment once ruled.

Yet for all our progress, much about the work experience hasn't changed in the past 50 years. People commute to work today the same as they did back then, except now they're likely to spend more time stuck in traffic.[2] Casual Fridays became casual every day at most companies, and you wouldn't want to own stock in a tie-making company. We became mobile, and mobility allowed some of us to work from home, but home quickly morphed into an Internet-wired coffee shop where a free outlet was as valuable as a pour-over demitasse of organic Jamaican Blue espresso. Everything changed and yet nothing changed. You still move to the Dallas office if that's where your employer tells you to go. The average office worker still spends 8 or 10 or 12 hours a day doing work in exchange for a paycheck, and then wakes up to the shriek of the alarm clock. You think you can't take it for another second and then you get up and do it again.

---

[2]Christopher Ingraham, "The astonishing human potential wasted on commutes," February 2016, https://www.washingtonpost.com/news/wonk/wp/2016/02/25/how-much-of-your-life-youre-wasting-on-your-commute/?utm_term=.1cc85ac0d87e.

The Internet was supposed to transform everything. Yet compare today's office worker to his or her 1965 counterpart. Apart from the fact that today's desk jockey uses a laptop instead of a typewriter and sends emails instead of printed memos, not much is different. Work was repetitive then and it's repetitive now. The stressed-out worker back then drank his share of martinis; today you'll find them taking Ashtanga yoga (and probably knocking back a craft cocktail afterwards: progress!). But work in 1965 involved repetitive tasks that fit snugly into a narrow box, and that's our work ethic today. The new world order was supposed to deliver a higher sense of fulfillment and meaning for today's professional. Instead we got cubicle culture and the expectation that we'd be at a manager's beck and call 24/7 given the small devices we carry around with us everywhere and every second. Weekend free time is a thing of the past. We're infinitely more likely to check email before we go to bed than any other number of activities that once used to be considered the platinum standard of our search for a meaningful existence.

* * *

The iconic work lament movie *Office Space* was released in 1999. But for a conspicuous lack of smartphones, it seems to spoof perfectly today's work world. Life is dreary for Peter Gibbons, the movie's protagonist. He works for a tech company and suffers the wounds of alienation. His managers hassle him for the mundane and ridiculous nits that we still associate with work today. As a programmer, Peter supposedly sits near the top of the work hierarchy, but work for him is nothing but a paycheck. His boss is smarmy and loathsome; he too is frustrated, unmotivated, and alienated. Peter and two coworkers are so miserable that they initiate a plot to commit corporate fraud as an escape route. The film portrays what a sad state of affairs the workplace has become, then and now.

The worker "becomes an appendage of the machine who must learn only the most simple, monotonous, most easily acquired knack," Karl Marx and Friedrich Engels wrote in *The Communist Manifesto*. The alarming part is that their words seem relevant to many talented people working in today's corporation. From Marx to *Office Space*, the typical professional worker's mission and purpose, along with free will, are still subjugated to those of the corporation—should they choose to stay trapped in a situation that makes them unhappy.

Polling confirms what most of us know: for too many people, work is a grind. Gallup has been studying workforce attitudes in the United States since 2012. Its most recent "State of the American Workplace" report revealed that 70 percent of people do not feel engaged at work.[3] Only 13 percent feel proud to work where they do. One in four admit that they are "actively disengaged," which Gallup defined as being so emotionally disconnected from the workplace that they were acting out on their unhappiness. In 2005, *The European Journal of Epidemiology* published a study that concluded that heart attack rates are lowest on weekends and then spike significantly on Mondays, when people return to work.[4] Work is literally killing us. Is it any wonder that so many of us are dissatisfied, Jacob Morgan asked in his book *The Future of Work*: "We have literally built our companies from the ground up with the notion that employees are just cogs and that work is drudgery."[5]

It would be easy to lower oneself into this well-documented, oft-written-about pit of corporate despair and throw in the towel. Plenty have before us. However, we are of a more optimistic bent, which brings us to what we think of as the potential for a fourth Industrial Revolution—as unveiled by the World Economic Forum

---

[3] http://Gallup, 2017, www.gallup.com/services/178514/state-american-workplace .aspx.

[4] Anahad O'Connor, "The Claim: Heart Attacks are more common on Mondays," March 14, 2016, www.nytimes.com/2006/03/14/health/14real.html.

[5] Jacob Morgan, *The Future of Work* (Hoboken, NJ: John Wiley & Sons, 2014), xiv.

in 2016. That would be the reinvention of work that removes the corporation from the center of things and reinserts the individual in its place. We spend such a large portion of our life at work, thinking about work, or stressed out because of work. It is the center of our universe, and technology has made it even more so. It's the one place (at least on an hours basis) where things like satisfaction and fulfillment should be paramount, and yet nothing could be further from that truth. Isn't it time to think about a new paradigm? For example, maybe the best place to work isn't the cubicle where you toil 50 weeks out of the year. How about an office you've designed for yourself in your own home? Or, if you are a person who needs some modicum of daily human interaction, what about one of the multiple coworking locations that are springing up in urban areas (and even suburban) around the country? Our worldview even allows for the individual who longs to go off grid and yet still stay gainfully employed. You really can move to that coastal village in Maine, buy that used lobster boat, and license a few dozen pots while still taking on a flexible corporate job that helps pay the bills.

It would be kind of like returning to the way it used to be 12,000 years ago, when the world was made up entirely of free agents and people managed to look out for themselves. Not that we were thinking about any of this in 2013, when we first came up with the idea that eventually became Catalant. But it strikes us as obvious now—just as it is to plenty of people outside corporate America and many forward-thinking people within. The world has moved forward, mainly enabled by technology. We've got the tools; we are only limited by our imagination and willpower. Are we really going to keep queuing up on the major freeways like the ghastly 405 and 495 and the Long Island Expressway, punching the clock, and wiling away the best years of our lives? There must be a better way to work.

CHAPTER **2**

HourlyNerd

The email hit our phones late one night while we were doing what first-year grad students do—namely, hanging out with one another. Sure, the grad school happened to be Harvard Business School, or HBS as we all referred to it, which came with its reputation, along with plenty of expectations.

The message was directed at the students who had yet to formally submit a team for the school's entrepreneurial face-off, the faux stock market competition. So right then and there, at Harvard Square landmark Tommy Doyle's (since departed), we assembled our six-person brain trust. It would be the three of us and three other friends from our section: Jose Pelaez,[1] who had worked for an energy start-up after earning a degree in chemical engineering at Columbia; Marshall Martin,[2] a Georgia Tech grad who had worked as an analyst at the consulting firm Accenture; and Kyle Snook,[3] a West Point grad who had served as a platoon leader in Afghanistan before enrolling at business school. At the time, it felt like an all-star roster to us. In retrospect, we probably should have given a little more thought to things like diversity of work experience and complementary skills when assembling our team. None of us knew much, if anything, about sales, marketing, or design. We had no experience in product management. We were friends. We enjoyed one another's company. So we became a team.

---

[1]https://www.linkedin.com/in/jose-pelaez-69509b7a.

[2]https://www.linkedin.com/in/marshall-martin-715bb343/

[3]https://www.linkedin.com/in/kyle-snook-b58b5399.

The first step was coming up with a concept for a business. And it had better be a winner, because whatever we dreamt up, we had to live with for the rest of the semester. Kyle suggested an application that would let people move down to better seats at sporting events. We all enjoyed a night at Fenway or the Garden, so we bandied that about. If you were stuck high up in the nosebleed section at Gillette Stadium, where the Patriots play, wouldn't you snap up a better seat if that were available? Made sense to us. Our proposed app would let you pay to sit closer to the action. In theory, both the sports venues and the teams that played there would embrace the idea because it would allow them to better optimize revenues. Unfortunately, we lacked the expertise to build even a rudimentary prototype. We decided that while the idea was a good one, we weren't the best people to pursue it. Next!

Boston was a notoriously cold place to be in the winter, so Pat suggested we sell what he called "nose bags," to be worn outside with your hat, muffler, and gloves on those really cold days. It was something he had seen during a play when he was younger: a small knit pouch held in place by a rope around the ears. The idea seemed so absurd as to be laughable, but it *was* a tangible product that vendors could sell, and we were running out of time. Pat offered an impassioned plea: "We'll push it like hell and win the competition by working harder than everybody else." No one could ever argue with Pat's contagious enthusiasm. Rob, however, who was probably the most serious and academic of us, hated the idea. The more he sputtered about the notion of selling a mitten for the face, the harder Pat pushed back. The fact that the product seemed so silly, he insisted, would make it that much sweeter when we took the grand prize. The idea died in committee.

As the night grew long and a cold, wintry walk home loomed, it didn't seem we were any closer to a solution. We might have gotten behind those nosebags if Rob wasn't so disgusted by the idea. In desperation, he shared with everyone a business plan he had secretly written the night before, for a concept called Rent-A-Nerd. He began to wax poetic about the concept, inspired by his father, who often asked Rob for on-demand pinch-hit finance help for his small company. Like many of our fathers' generation, and despite having an MBA from Harvard and a long career of business success, Rob's father had found that recent financial modeling technology changed too quickly to stay current. We had grown up on the stuff, and we were used to our elders turning to us for help. In Rob's case, it might take him 30 minutes to work up a spreadsheet that could take his father far longer. What if we matched up young, skilled, hungry grad students like ourselves with small business people and business owners who were as in the dark about this newfangled stuff as Rob's dad was? Not everyone tasked with running his own firm has a son or daughter who has worked as an analyst for Goldman Sachs. Why not build a matchmaking site to help small businesses gain access to MBA and business graduates who possess the same skills as expensive consultants but cost a lot less? The other five of us snapped into reality. Did this have legs?

Each of us had at least some direct exposure to the tried, true, and inefficient system we call the consulting industry. Two of us had cut our teeth prior to grad school working for large corporations that were regular customers of blue chip consulting firms. These lucrative arrangements most definitely worked for the consulting firm partners, who were paid exorbitant amounts for their services. However, the deal rarely worked out for those on the purchasing side of the equation. The consulting firms' pricing was opaque, and the black-box services they provided were often ill-defined. About the only thing that was clear was that the big firms were paid a lot, no matter the quality of their deliverables, which only sometimes included recommendations that might even help people who had hired them make an actual decision.

Pat had worked on the supply side—he was a consultant himself for a few years—which meant he got to witness the absurdities firsthand. As one of the young recruits in the trenches, he was paid the equivalent of around 30 bucks an hour. The dirty little secret, of course, is that in the consulting industry it's common to bill closer to $500 an hour (and far more for senior resources). What's more, there was seemingly little quality control or accountability to the clients who were forking out the big bucks. Pat was a generalist, but he was frequently hired out to provide expertise he didn't have in industries he didn't know. The client would pay an inflated rate just for the time it took Pat to get up to speed. Confounding matters even more, his first assignments as a consultant seemed to have no purpose. If there was a working business model here, Pat was not privy to it. Later, after jumping to a boutique firm in Boston, he had a much healthier experience, but even then it revealed segments of a model desperately in need of fixing. While he had the utmost respect for the partner he worked with, he also saw that he spent most of his time selling work, rather than actually doing it, which is what he most enjoyed and thought he had signed on for. Based on Pat's experience, along with Rob's observation that people like his father could benefit from a pool of highly trained talent, it seemed like the $100-billion-a-year consulting industry might well be ripe for disruption. The question was: Where do we begin?

Some on the team had reservations. Creating a marketplace would prove a huge challenge, especially given the limited time we had for the assignment. Add to that, none of us knew the first thing about creating or designing a website, which would be the obvious first step toward creating the company. For that matter, none of us had any experience in selling, marketing, or any of the other skill sets we would need to pull off what we were describing. There were also the limits placed on us by the class guidelines. We had less than three months to prove the viability of our concept. And we had a limited budget of $5,000 to pull it all off. Even if we spent some of our up-front money paying someone to build our website, that would take time. So would populating a marketplace that would require explaining what we had in mind to every potential consultant or customer we could scare up between classes. The challenges were daunting, to say the least. But in the end, we liked the idea. It surely beat the nosebags by a length. We figured we could fake it 'til we made it.

Of course the birth of Rent-A-Nerd was an unmitigated flop when we presented it to the class. Along with our epic disorganization and Scrooge McDuck graphics, we at least knew enough to throw in a slide noting the size of the consulting industry and the opportunity to bite into it, should we ever actually figure out what we were doing. Looking back, we can see we did so poorly in the bake-off that day in part because of the brash optimism of our concept. We were young upstarts in a sea of young upstarts, professing that we had something no one else did that could change the world. That was bound to draw a strong reaction—more so than if you're with the team that claims they're going to sell the perfect reversible belt (one side brown, the other black!). The same held true for all those T-shirt companies and other more conventional business ideas pitched that day. In contrast, we were trying to sell our fellow students on a company that we claimed could take a big bite of business from the very same consulting firms that at least some hoped would employ them after graduation. And it didn't help that we couldn't even answer the most basic questions about a company like ours with such bold ambitions. Basically, we put ourselves squarely in the firing line. You can't hate a reversible belt—but you can have a visceral reaction to someone who says they are going to destroy your future chosen industry!

As our rollout started gaining steam, we were forced to look inward and figure out why we were doing this in the first place. One of us had initially looked on the start-up competition as simply a part of graduating from school. He was going to spend his career optimizing the workings of established businesses, not start one of his own. Rather than a potentially life-altering event, he saw the class at first as part of the educational experience. Rob had been focused on starting a company when applying to business school, but by the time he entered four years later, he had self-selected out of the start-up scene. Lacking computer skills and creativity, he didn't see himself as Silicon Valley material. He might have had the right skills to serve as an early stage manager but certainly didn't fancy himself someone to start something big. Rob was also the practical sort, the kind of grounded, rational guy who simply couldn't help but run the numbers. And when he did, the odds of survival were long. For every Facebook or Airbnb, there were probably a thousand failures. Ten thousand. A hundred thousand! And even the rare success had to be viewed with a healthy dose of skepticism. All wins are not created equal. For every Mark Zuckerberg, there are hundreds more entrepreneurs still running a company they started—except instead of sexy Facebook or Instagram, it's a regional manufacturing concern chugging along with an app that tracks boxcars, or a new piece of technology that can attach buttons to shirts on the line in Vietnam more efficiently. Rob had arrived at Harvard sponsored by Bain Capital, and was very excited by returning to the firm that had treated him so well and he had enjoyed so much. Never far from the front of his mind, Pitch Day and the subsequent race to the bottom began as a class exercise, not a life's pursuit.

Peter arrived at business school seeking to move into an operating role at a non-financial firm—a departure from his short career to that point. Like Rob, he didn't feel prepared to start a company and was dubious about the risk-reward tradeoff at this point in his life. His general aversion to risk—something that made him valuable as an offsetting complement to Rob and Pat over time—made him a skeptic. Peter viewed the start-up competition as a means to an end: graduating business school and moving on to the next step in his career.

Pat was the most entrepreneurial among us, but he was also the most dubious about the utility of this start-up experiment to prove much of anything. As constructed on paper, companies that racked up quick, short-term sales would be rewarded, while those building for the long-term would be devalued. There might be some valuable lessons woven into this exercise, but it did not play to his higher consciousness. One day, Pat surmised, he might start a company based on something that moved him with people he cared about. But he wasn't ready. He still had more to learn. And he was convinced you need a perfectly formed, well thought-out idea before jumping into the start-up waters.

Looking back on our underwhelming cache of product confidence, one might argue that out of the gate we were not exactly the go-to model for start-up success. Still, ranking 150th out of 150 in our class competition got under our skin. It really needled us. So maybe our presentation skills at the early stage were lacking. Coming in last lit a fire under us. It changed everything.

We put that chip on our shoulder into sheer man hours, spending every last minute of free time pushing Rent-A-Nerd, which, because the domain name wasn't available, we renamed HourlyNerd. At that point, we were six people going on three. We divvied up assignments, but it was clear that Jose, Marshall, and Kyle were less excited about the idea than we were. As the semester unspooled and the workload accelerated, they confessed that they were lukewarm. They were looking to help work on a class project but were less excited about dedicating all available time to the idea.

Our task list grew even as our ranks thinned. We needed to find someone to build the website while simultaneously doing those things that professors expect when you're still in business school: for example, demonstrating proof points of concept. We fumbled for a few days seeking email lists of small companies but quickly realized the only way to test our idea was to talk with actual human beings. So we became door-to-door salesmen and took HourlyNerd to the street. We found talkers, which was a long cry from takers when it came down to it. It was easy for a small business owner to say he was open to quality consulting help from young experts, but would he actually be willing to part with some of his hard-earned cash to make it happen? We needed to sell business owners on the wisdom of signing up for our service and then convince them to post projects on our site. We also needed to recruit our "Nerds"—the MBA students and recent business school grads we imagined scouring through our website and then bidding on the jobs that theoretically would appear out of thin air.

In order to find these Nerds, our idea was to print up what we called "Nerdy Bucks"—regular-sized dollar bills with our logo in place of George Washington's head. A goofy idea for a give-away for sure, but then again, it was brought to you by the people who thought Scrooge McDuck was a compelling sales figure. Emboldened by our newfound passion and complete lack of shame, we printed out the phony bills that would double as flyers and then proceeded to hand them out while loitering around the halls of MIT's Sloan School of Management and the Questrom School of Business at Boston University. (One of the rules of our in-class competition was that we couldn't involve our fellow students in the business. No one said anything about the rest of the hungry Boston graduate student population.) Our pitch was straightforward: "Hey, we started this company. Do you wanna make a few extra bucks?" We got some hostile pushback right out of the gate because people thought we had tricked them into checking out our brilliant opportunity by handing out fake money. Mostly we got ignored. It really made you feel for the sandwich board folks who still stroll the streets of Boston and New York hawking everything from bike tours to chicken nugget samples. There's thankless work, then there's thankless work. As we plied the streets, maybe 1 in 10 would hear us out. "Hey, dude! You can make a hundred dollars an hour helping small businesses in the area with cool projects." *Uh-huh.* We reached out to friends we had at other top-tier business schools: Dartmouth's Tuck School of Management, Northwestern's Kellogg School of Management, the Wharton School at the University of Pennsylvania. Perseverance has its virtues. By the end of the semester, more than 550 MBAs had signed up on our site.

The other half of the equation proved a much bigger challenge. Finding businesses to keep these Nerds busy took up the bulk of those 500 or so hours each of us put into the company while it was still a class project. When meeting with potential business owners we hoped to sign up, we talked about them paying $50 an hour for our service, not a few hundred. For that very reasonable fee, you would gain access to the kind of pointy-headed MBAs who would soon be out of reach once they began working for the blue-chip firms and Fortune 1000 companies that would greedily scoop them up after graduation. We thought the price break made sense, but even $50 an hour seemed high to the people we were selling. Professional managers in the world of corporate finance were a world apart from the small business owners, who would be paying that fee from their own pockets.

Usually we worked in pairs. Each afternoon after class and on weekends we'd take turns donning a blazer and khakis and walking into nearby businesses to sell them on our idea. We started with the storefronts near the business school, which is located in Boston, across the Charles River from the university's main campus in Cambridge. We methodically moved to the bars, restaurants, and shops on and around Harvard Square and then pounded the pavement in the surrounding neighborhoods. We hit laundromats and salons, pizza shops and yoga studios. We eventually branched out into professional-looking services—anything with a storefront office or a shingle hanging from a second floor. This was probably not what our parents imagined when they agreed to help us pay for our continuing education at America's most renowned institute of higher learning. We heard a lot of "no's." Occasionally we heard more than just no. "Get out!" the owner of one diner yelled at us, except in more colorful language, forcefully delivered in the local dialect. Sometimes, when we did not read the tea leaves quickly enough, we found ourselves running steps ahead of an angry shop owner clattering out of his property's front door.

You can't say we didn't learn anything from our early forays into sales and marketing. Lesson No. 1: lose the blazers, or at least sound a little bit less like the business school students that we were. There are some built-in prejudices to what we were doing, so the least we could do is not look the role that our detractors accused us of being.

Through trial and error we quickly learned that selling something as esoteric as the professional consulting services of an MBA student required more than a fake dollar bill and our rose-colored-glasses pitch. Our "MBA services" needed to be repackaged, and pronto. The clock was ticking. We came upon a new plan. Instead of hawking a generic suite of services, what if we figured out these potential customers' pain points and sold solutions to those? "Do you need someone who can work up ideas for an inexpensive marketing campaign to draw more customers? What about some new ideas for your social media strategy? Don't have one yet? Maybe we can help!"

Salvation arrived in the last place we would have expected. Veggie Galaxy, a burrito joint on Central Square in Cambridge, was nestled between a cacophony of bustling, student-oriented food establishments. The first time we walked in was on a Saturday around lunchtime. Every other place on the square was packed. There were maybe two people in the Veggie Galaxy. We asked for the manager, who turned out to be the owner as well. Perfect. If ever there was a company that needed some marketing help, this was the place. We introduced ourselves and cut to the chase. "Your business is lacking customers. What if we could give you low-price access to experts who could devise a marketing strategy that gets some of those people off the street and into your establishment?" The owner practically jumped. "Oh my god, I need help," he confessed. As it turned out, he had hired someone through Craigslist who billed himself as a marketing wiz and left him wondering if the guy even knew how to spell hashtag. The so-called consultant had set him back a week's worth of inventory and barely made a dent in his lackluster business returns.

We tried not to step on each other's toes in our enthusiasm to ring up the sale. This poor guy's story could cut one of two ways. He'd either realize that we were the real deal, offering him a valid solution, or he could chase us straight out the door. Pat, who had a real workingman's knowledge and ability to read his audience, opened up his laptop and forged ahead. "I know you're on a budget, but I know you want the best people," he began. "Our people have worked at places like Goldman Sachs and McKinsey. They've worked as analysts at top private equity funds." Pat called up the resume of one of our preselected Nerds and invited the owner to peer over his shoulder. "This guy's got three years at Proctor & Gamble and now he's at Dartmouth's Tuck." Pat paused, dramatically, giving the owner a moment to ponder. "Think you could work with someone like this?" The next words the owner uttered would ring in Pat's ears for years to come, whenever anyone expressed doubts about our company. "I would pay anything to get that person! When can they start?"

We learned some valuable lessons from this exchange. One, know your customer. Pat rightly read that this gentleman would appreciate the level of expertise we were offering, and yet he didn't talk down to him. Others might want different examples. Pat got this one exactly right.

Second, understand pain. Many small businesses were desperate, or at least this one certainly was. Understand the product you are selling and what you can do to help someone with real needs. With our company, we had figured out the broad outlines for a platform that allows small business owners real-time access to the talent they need to solve their problems. At the outset, we had focused on price when imagining the lure of our platform. Now we realized that quick turnaround could also be a selling point. Learn how to dance on a dime when you are making your pitch.

Our experience on the street was illustrating what our greatest challenge was going to be. Nerds were relatively easy to come by, but customers were a whole different ballgame. Despite our enthusiasm to quickly scale the business, we still had the day job of classes to attend and in fact, there were still competitors vying for first place on "IPO Day," as the school dubbed the final competition among the student ventures.

In early May of 2012, the entire first-year class gathered across 10 rooms in Aldrich Hall, the business school's core first-year classroom building, where the process of crowning the ultimate winner would begin. Each team was given 10 minutes to make the case that its company was the most promising of the 15 founded by those of us in Section F. This time we were prepared. Three months earlier, we had no clue if businesses would even want what we were selling. We didn't know if MBA students had the time or inclination to sign up for our service. But now we had retained nearly 250 businesses, and roughly 100 of them had already posted a project. We could also say with certainty that we would have no trouble bringing experts, or "Nerds," onboard. More than 500 MBAs had already signed up at the site.

At that point, we were describing HourlyNerd as a "cloud-based talent management platform." Pretty generic tech-speak, in retrospect, but fortunately we had real numbers to back up our talk. There were 27.9 million small businesses in the United States at the start of the 2010s, generating $7.8 trillion in annual revenues. We needed only to capture a small sliver of those dollars to build a sizable business. A shift in our business model now meant that we were collecting a fee on both sides of the equation: a 10 percent share of every deal a business consummated on our site, along with a 5 percent cut of the MBA's payday. We spoke of expanding our offering by reaching into engineering and design schools and laid out other potential new revenue streams (resume sales, advertising) that we would end up never pursuing. We cited a model we had run that showed us generating $100 million just from the MBA vertical inside of five years.

Maybe we just imagined the nods as we looked around the room. We had not forgotten how foolish we came off looking the first time out of the gate. This time felt different. Maybe our business model was resonating precisely because the room was full of former consultants and those who had worked for companies that spilled millions every year on consulting services for no clear payoff.

As IPO Day unfolded, the other teams resorted to an abundance of slick videos and multimedia tools to tout their companies. We chose a more traditional approach and let the numbers do the talking. The school's 150 teams had collectively earned roughly $16,000 in revenue over the semester. We had generated just under $9,000 of those dollars, and we were boldly predictive of the fact we could have done a lot better. "The Field 3 funding parameters severely limit our ability to build out the requisite technological sophistication, which has prevented us from closing more business," we wrote in the three-page pitch we had worked up for the final day of the competition. If we had been allowed to spend the money to build a better functioning, more professional-looking website, we figured we would have booked closer to $20,000 in revenue. We had started off the class as our make-believe stock market's worst performing equity. Every company had an opening price of $100 and we had hit a low of $32. We ended the semester trading at $351 a share—the class's top-performing stock.

Outside judges, including professors, local venture capitalists (VCs), and prominent alumni, had been brought in to declare the winner in each section. We were psyched about our performance, but guardedly optimistic after we won the first round of judging. There was a 30-minute break and then the entire class gathered in the school auditorium for the final face-off among the 10 section winners. There was a reality show vibe to the whole affair. The first-place finisher would be determined by both the audience—our fellow students—and the judges. The audience would count for half the vote, the judges the other half.

Waiting to present in front of more than 900 people, we felt a combination of excitement, dread, and nausea. The business was demanding more and more of our time, and yet we still had to keep up with our work for other classes. We were burning the candle practically around the clock. As the finals proceeded, the three of us were operating on adrenalin, Dunkin' Donuts coffee, and little else.

We were the last group to present. There were other strong contenders, including an app created to help people deal remotely with an ailing parent. That struck us as a clever and worthy idea, but from a strictly commercial standpoint, it didn't seem to have the moneymaking potential to claim the grand prize. Other businesses got up on stage and clearly knew how to present: they employed slick marketing techniques and a lot of savvy, but to our minds that was mostly smoke and not so much fire—all intended to distract the judges from their team's lack of revenues. Ours was the most unapologetically commercial of all the ideas presented, which presumably would serve us well inside a business school. Despite our nerves and lack of sleep, when it was finally our turn on stage, we turned it on and felt we hit it out of the park. As the judges conferred, we felt so bullish about our chances that Pat was already talking about his trip to the tattoo parlor that he had promised if we won.

The student vote flashed up on-screen. We ended up taking a very close second to the ailing parent concept. Maybe that was inevitable. Ours was a boring business-to-business (B-to-B) proposition up against a trendy app aimed at a clearly sympathetic and much broader consumer market. Still, we thought we had a chance to play catch-up and sweep the vote among the investors, entrepreneurs, and other like-minded capitalist/judges. The grand finale arrived. No deal. We ended up taking second place, even among the judges.

We knew we should have been proud. Taking second out of 150 teams was a great accomplishment. At the very least, Pat should have been relieved that he wouldn't be walking around for the rest of his life with the company logo tattooed on his butt. We felt keenly disappointed. On the other hand, we had another motivator to stoke the fires burning within each of us: to prove that our classmates and the judges had made a mistake.

There was a reception for the top three teams immediately following the contest, but Pat was so angry over the second-place finish that he didn't want to go. Rob cajoled him with the inducement of a free dinner and limitless upside of mingling with successful HBS alumni. Besides, we reasoned, if nothing else, it was a chance to meet the judges.

It's a good thing we did. Once there, Pat settled back into his usual congenial and gregarious self, which in no small part contributed to him meeting a man named Bob Doris. Doris was an HBS grad himself, who had recently sold—for nearly $800 million—the technology company he and his wife had cofounded in the 1980s. He was now an active angel investor who liked spending time on campus in search of interesting young start-ups. He had been one of the judges in our section and also had judged the school-wide competition.

"I thought you guys should have won," Bob confided to Pat. We didn't argue with him. Bob was now based in the San Francisco Bay

Area and had a front-row seat to the rise of the gig economy. He told us he saw potential in our project for an online marketplace for a different (higher-end) segment of the labor force. "I think you have a real business here," he said. He gave us his card and told us if we were ever in the Bay Area, we should look him up. We played it cool—Pat said something about how we were probably going to bootstrap it for a while. We had a few thousand dollars in our coffers. None of us were clear on what the future might hold for HourlyNerd. But we'd put this much time and sweat equity into the project. We had a second-place ribbon and now a contact in the Silicon Valley. Why not make a fund-raising trip to California? Who was to say our little boondoggle might not be the pot of gold at the end of the VC rainbow?

CHAPTER 3

The Gig Economy

In May of 2013—around the same time we were preparing for the IPO Day competition—Clayton M. Christensen held a roundtable discussion at HBS about the disruption of the professional services industry. Professor Christensen, who authored *The Innovator's Dilemma*, was probably the most renowned professor on the business school faculty. His theory of disruptive innovation has practically given rise to a cottage industry. By that point, he and two colleagues, Dina Wang and Derek van Bever, had interviewed more than 50 people on the topic, including those with established firms, upstarts, clients, and researchers. He narrowed his focus to two areas. One was legal services. The other was the world of consulting—the same realm we were bumping up against with HourlyNerd.

"We have come to the conclusion that the same forces that disrupted so many businesses, from steel to publishing, are starting to reshape the world of consulting,"[1] Christensen, Wang, and van Bever would write in a paper published in the *Harvard Business Review* that fall. Professor Christensen himself had put in his time in big consulting when he worked earlier in his career for the Boston Consulting Group. (He had also worked in Washington for two years as a special assistant to the U.S. Secretary of Transportation and in the 1980s cofounded a ceramics company called CPS Technologies.) He recognized in consulting an industry that

---

[1] https://hbr.org/2013/10/consulting-on-the-cusp-of-disruption.

hadn't changed its fundamental business model in more than 100 years. It was ripe for disruption.

The most elite tier of the management consulting industry consisted of the Big Three: McKinsey & Company, Bain & Company, and the Boston Consulting Group. Those three out-fits alone generated $15 billion a year in revenues. Modest-sized projects involved teams of no fewer than six people. A three-month engagement could cost a business as much as $2 million, and it wasn't uncommon for a Fortune 100 company to spend as much as $100 million per year on their services. The wider management consulting industry in the United States was roughly three times that size. Worldwide, it amounted to more than $100 billion in revenues annually.[2] These firms were prized for their outsider's perspective and the wide experience they presumably brought to the job. But typically it was the more junior generalists who did the lion's share of the work, not the seasoned partner who had landed the account. The hours were grueling and the turnover crazy—as much as 20 percent a year inside the big firms, despite all the money they spent on training and perks. That was bad news for the Big Three but good news for us. It potentially meant a larger pool of Nerds to pursue. McKinsey alone had 27,000 alumni,[3] according to data Christensen's research group had released. Among the Big Three, that number was approaching 50,000.

Exacerbating the problem for the top consulting firms was the fact that there is often an inverse relationship between the value of the employees who leave and those who stay. The most coveted are those who depart—because they can. What if HourlyNerd became a platform for the consulting world's most coveted talent—those who had the moxie and skill to venture off on their own?

---

[2]https://www.statista.com/statistics/466460/global-management-consulting-market-size-by-sector/.

[3]https://hbr.org/2013/10/consulting-on-the-cusp-of-disruption.

While we sensed a burgeoning talent opportunity through our pursuit of these wayward bodies, the brain trust behind the Big Three were not so quick to acquiesce. They explained to Christensen and the other investigators that their industry was different. They offered a specialized expertise that businesses couldn't get anywhere else and could not be commoditized. Besides, why should the Big Three choose to change their ways, except perhaps incrementally (read: invisible baby steps that made no difference to anyone, least of all in costs to companies and billable hours for the consultants) when things were going so well for the industry? Christensen and his colleagues had heard it all before. "If our long study of disruption has led us to any universal conclusion," he reported, "it is that every industry will eventually face it. New competitors with new business models arrive; incumbents choose to ignore the new players or flee to higher-margin activities; a disrupter whose product was once barely good enough achieves a level of quality acceptable to the broad middle of the market, undermining the position of longtime leaders and often causing the 'flip' to a new basis of competition."[4]

It sounded like good news to us. We wouldn't get a mention in Christensen's original piece. We were founded too recently and still too small at that point to merit one. But we got a nice consolation prize that might have been just as valuable. Dina Wang, one of the paper's cowriters, published a blog post at the HBR website under the headline "Revenge of the Hourly Nerds."[5] "Think of it as eLance for consultants instead of programmers, writers and designers, or as eBay for consulting problems," she wrote.

We didn't know Dina, whose bio indicated she had put in her time at McKinsey. She observed that, like so many disruptive

---

[4]Clayton M. Christensen, Dina Wang, and Derek van Bever, October 2014 issue, page 1, https://hbr.org/2013/10/consulting-on-the-cusp-of-disruption.

[5]Dina Wang, Revenge of the Hourly Nerds, Sep. 18, 2013, https://hbr.org/2013/09/revenge-of-the-hourlynerds.

businesses, we were entering at the industry's basement door and targeting the small concerns that the big consulting firms didn't care about. "These are clients for whom HourlyNerd is a godsend," she wrote, "because they want the consulting help but can't afford the hefty consulting fees of traditional firms."

The desire to leave the basement is inevitable, Dina continued. "Will HourlyNerd, like many other disruptors across industries, want to move up-market to bigger and bigger clients, attracted by the greater profits those relationships promise?" She laid out other possible pitfalls, including the instinct to move beyond the top MBA programs to expand our pool of potential Nerds. That might let us keep up with demand, she said, but there was also the risk that doing so would dilute our brand and value proposition. Interesting. She had our attention—but mainly we were just tickled that people were even noticing our tiny little company.

* * *

Airbnb's founders were simply trying to generate some extra income by renting out space on their floor. Now, of course, companies like Airbnb and its brethren in the sharing or gig economy are synonymous with disruption and shorthand for anyone talking about using mobile technology to disrupt or create a new field. Not now, and not even in our earliest days, have we ever deigned to inherit that mantel. Still, we know people out there who are describing us as the TaskRabbit of the consulting world—the potential matchmaker between business school alumni talent and the millions of small businesses that could use their services. We didn't start out imagining that the CEO of a 100-person corporation would whip out a phone to find the nearest MBA and offer that person a $20,000 a contract to solve a business problem. But it was inspiring just the same, starting with the relative frictionless of our potential marketplace.

It wasn't just companies like Airbnb and TaskRabbit that had our attention back then. Any number of companies making the radar screen were also proving to be inspiring. There was Lyft, willing to go head to head with Uber. The retail food, prep, and delivery business was cutting into the grocery store model. Instacart materialized to find work for those willing to shop on behalf of busy people at stores like Whole Foods, Safeway, Costco, and Target. Handy had created online platforms that let people sell their labor to those looking for movers, cleaners, or someone handy around the house. DoorDash launched an app that lets you hire a courier to deliver a package to someone locally—from the sweater your sister left when she was visiting over the weekend to a set of urgent legal papers that need signatures.

Pick an industry. Companies aimed at disrupting the labor market were sprouting like pop-ups. At the beginning, we were just surfing the disruption tide along with everyone else. However, there were differences between what we were starting versus the others. One, we were selling our service to businesses, while the rest of the headline-makers sold mainly to consumers. Another big difference was the world in which we hunted for talent. The Lyft driver or TaskRabbit handyman could come from a multitude of backgrounds, and a college degree was not prerequisite for entry. By contrast and by definition, virtually every one of our 40,000-plus experts has one. More than half of our Nerds have successfully completed a graduate program, and 5,000 have an MBA from a top five business program. Eventually, we'd add JDs, MDs, and a lot of PhDs. Over 10,000 of our experts have worked for a Fortune 500 company. Whereas the typical gig workers of the world were performing more basic tasks, our experts were typically selling their knowledge. Which, by the way, is not to say that some of them didn't choose to rent out a room or drive extra hours to round out their annual earnings. Being school smart didn't make you a snob. But HourlyNerd was offering a significantly higher rate, which was a big differentiator to the appeal of our platform as it came onboard in the growing gig economy.

A third difference between these varying workforces was the stakes. Today, there are a dozen or more companies offering the same opportunity to drive on-demand for a living. However, a business customer entrusting HourlyNerd with its inner sanctum is putting a lot on the line. The Nerd who under-delivers or blows it on a consulting gig may never be entrusted with a top assignment again. And the customer who suffers the pain of bad or faulty knowledge work is not coming back. The whole transaction is just a larger, weightier proposition, and that raised the bar on our responsibility, across the board.

Yet no matter how much of the gig economy–denying we engaged in, there were obvious parallels, starting with a similarity in vision. It had become evident to us that we were witnessing the birth of a workplace nation where there were ultimately going to be a lot more independent contractors than those who receive a bi-weekly paycheck from a single employer. A dozen years ago, gig economy participants were called freelancers, and to the average person that meant a writer, a musician, or an artist—or, similarly, a landscaper, a waiter, or a craftsperson. There was almost an artistic or creative underpinning to being a part of the freelance economy. No one associated it with a blazer and Macbook. We, however, did. That was our pivot point.

We recognized there were potentially big profits for those who could successfully navigate this new gig economy, but there were also pitfalls to be faced in execution. For one, we correctly assumed that for customers, trust was a big factor for all of us playing in the flexible on-demand arena, whether one sold to businesses or to consumers. The ratings system seemed like a big win for the business-to-consumers (B-to-C) model, such as Airbnb. This generation had been raised on "likes" for Facebook and reviews on Yelp. We were accustomed to weighing in and fighting back. That helped us think through potential solutions for our budding B-to-B.

If nothing else, these other companies' newfound success in creating labor markets in other spheres fueled our interest to turn a school project into a viable business. We weren't thinking we were about to turn the employment world upside down on its head. At least not yet. But if marketplaces could blossom for drivers and home cleaners, why not for MBAs and engineers, architects and graphic designers? Professionals in the skilled labor workforce can desire flexibility and control over their work as much as the next guy. But how were they expected to find the assignments they need to live, untethered from a single employer?

Today's workforce is much better educated than it was, even just a generation ago. Today, 4 in every 10 workers (39 percent) has a bachelor's degree, compared to 27 percent 20 years ago. Union membership has dropped 40 percent in just 30 years, helping to encourage this idea that we're all free agents. The year before we started grad school, Reid Hoffman of LinkedIn fame published a book called *The Startup of You*. "All humans are entrepreneurs," he declared. We're not 100 percent sure we agree with that sentiment, but we'd be happy if a lot more people recognized that working for themselves could be a path to a more fulfilling life—even if it is a life filled with bumps and uncertainty.

Stability is one of the foundational challenges we knew we were going to come up against as we attempted to build our stable of experts. Steady employ is perhaps the single largest reason people continue to work for a company despite how much they dislike it. In our parents' generation, it sufficed until a gold watch was served up for a lifetime of service. More recently, people stamped the clock because large companies offered benefits that seemed unobtainable unless you were lucky enough to land with the very best. But what if mobility and new technology could help highly trained workers land as much work as they liked, or could handle, without losing all the other benefits?

* * *

When we weren't sprinting to build HourlyNerd, we were still HBS students, and in addition to our classroom learning, it was hard not to observe the change coming about the country and among our peer group. Workers of all varieties were feeling restless. There was this sense in the air that there had to be a better way. What's more, from the employer side, the drumbeat of a perpetually receding gap between available talent and commercial needs continued growing louder and louder.

In 2010, Intuit, the financial software company, published a report that predicted that by 2020, approximately 40 percent of the country's workforce will be working as a freelancer, a temp worker, or a contractor. That translates to roughly 60 million Americans. Self-proclaimed thought leaders were offering, in their oracle-like fashion, pronouncements about moving along a "life path" rather than a "career path" and how, ultimately, most of us will end up serving as brand managers for ourselves. We were imagining a nation of dynamic free agents at a time people were feeling less tethered than ever before to their place of work. The very concept of work seemed to be changing.[6]

The broader economy is also transforming. Professor Joseph Fuller at HBS would teach us about the "demand/supply imbalance" he had noticed in the labor market. The 2008 Great Recession destroyed jobs for those with less education, his research found, and created millions of jobs for the well educated. Now, ours is an economy experiencing the pain of replacing manufacturing with service jobs, when even factory jobs increasingly require some college, if not a full-fledged degree. A favorite slide Professor Fuller liked to show picked up from the research arm of McKinsey, known as its Global Institute. The graphic projected that in the near future, the United States could have as many as

---

[6]Intuit, October 2010, p. 21, https://httpdownload.intuit.com/http.intuit/CMO/intuit/futureofsmallbusiness/intuit_2020_report.pdf.

1.5 million too few workers with a college or graduate degree, and nearly 6 million too many who have not completed high school. Throughout history, employees have traditionally been forced to adapt to an organization. But given the supply and demand curves, managers and organizations were now seeing the need to adapt to employees. And employees were what we projected we could provide in large supply.

Demographic changes were also working in our favor. As millennials, we represent one-third of the workforce and of course our share will only increase from there. A snapshot of millennials offered by Deloitte, the accounting giant, underscored the many ways that the attitudes of our broader demographic will help the HourlyNerd cause. Millennials are restless; only 16 percent see themselves at their current job a decade from now. Millennials are also not anxious to commute; three-quarters of them would like to work remotely. Deloitte's survey shows we put a priority on being in control of our own career path and feel empowered to pursue work that gives us flexibility. Nearly 9 in 10 respondents insisted that a business "should be measured by something more than just its financial success." Millennials care about the financial benefits of a job, of course, but Deloitte found that we're far more likely to follow a path that allows for a better work/life balance than previous generations.

Were we so bold as to think we'd invented this trend, we'd expect to be roundly criticized, if not hung out to dry. We were merely blazing a trail following pioneers who had recognized the needs of the temporary workforce long before we hauled our duffel bags onto the campus in Boston. Kelly Services is a name synonymous with temporary employ. First known for its staffing of people in the office environment since 1946, the company has updated and grown with the times. It has repeatedly branched out and today engages more than 500,000 people across all services and industries. We originally saw Kelly as a competitor but later realized they were the perfect potential partner. What if our unique platform and their menu of services could be complementary to the cause of providing more people the right to work as they please? Could this be the wave of the future?

Information technology (IT)—always considered a disrupter—has also been a leader in adopting the needs of its workforce. Easily parodied at times, despite its foosball mentality and cubicle-free environment, the IT industry has become a bastion of liberation, serving the needs of its people, rather than the other way around. We can only expect that the tide will continue to rise for the flexible worker as IT growth continues to permeate our society.

That is not to say that every company is going to be swept up in a tsunami of mass exodus followed by the quadrupling of the WeWork economy. TaskRabbit is not going to put Dow Chemical out of business, and no matter how many ride-sharing cars line the queues at airports, we'll still need airlines to buy, fill, and fly the planes. Some businesses are more ripe for disruption than others. It seems likely that for as long as we have a post office, there will be postal workers. Government is notoriously slow and unwieldy to change, but maybe there is creature-comfort in that. The Morgan Stanleys, Fords and Honeywells still need to put people behind desks and on the line, and we suspect they are going to be around for a while. We don't pretend to suggest that every last worker born after 1998 is going to swear off a traditional job. We need companies that have infrastructure that support a hybrid workforce. But those companies also need to adapt to the needs and desires of a changing worker dynamic. In starting HourlyNerd, we believed there was a place for a full-time workforce as well as the flexible expert worker who helicopters in and provides value. The two should be able to coexist. But before we could stake our claim to stewardship of the millennial psyche, first we had to convince some large companies that our ideas had freight and relevance. Otherwise our whole idea could go up in smoke as little more than a second-place finisher in an HBS classroom exercise.

CHAPTER **4**

Walking Sand Hill Road

Companies are always seeking to become more economical and more efficient; Catalant is a tool for getting to that next frontier of efficiency and effectiveness.

—JOSEPH FULLER, PROFESSOR OF MANAGEMENT, HBS

We completed our first year of business school in May of 2013. By mid-June we would be working at the summer jobs we had prearranged long before any of us had recognized the full potential of HourlyNerd. That gave us barely a month to devote ourselves full time to our company without the numerous distractions of school, summer employ, friends, and family. HourlyNerd had occupied a new and urgent spot in our lives, and we felt compelled to take this ride for as far as it would get us. We coordinated schedules, found a clear slot, and booked flights to the West Coast for the end of May. In our usual fly-by-the-seat-of-our-pants fashion, we had our air tickets before we had so much as a single meeting lined up. Hence, task number one was sending emails to any and every HBS grad we could think of—anyone with whom we could claim a whiff of a connection—working for a Silicon Valley venture firm. Keeping in mind the continuing frenzy of start-up fever, this was akin to getting a tip on the winning horse at the Kentucky Derby.

We hit the phones and texts and were shockingly able to land a few dozen meetings, largely via alumni connections from our colleges and HBS. After a manic week with pitch after pitch, we didn't get a single bite. Some VCs were kind and generous, some brusque and rude, but all meetings ended the same way.

It's amazing how many variations there are of the word "no." Still, we thought there was a chance we had our original Boston advocate, Bob Doris, in our back pocket when we crossed the Golden Gate Bridge in our economy rental car. The thick green foliage of Marin County never looked so welcoming as we GPS-ed our way to the one person we hoped was interested in investing in our company. We knew we were hanging our hat on a lot. If Bob Doris changed his mind about taking a flyer with three people he barely knew from the East Coast, then maybe it was time to consider throwing in the bag.

Bob had cut his teeth in the consulting business at the start of his career. He had been on the periphery of the Bay Area tech scene since the 1980s and in recent years had watched the rise of the on-demand companies that rely on free agents. He had already been viewing the consulting industry as one ripe for disintermediation by the time he saw our pitch for HourlyNerd back in Boston. He immediately understood the potential of a gig economy business that aimed at so fat a target.

Bob himself had been something of an accidental entrepreneur. He had gone to Harvard undergrad and then stayed to earn both his JD and MBA in a joint degree program in law and business. He took a job as a strategist in the Menlo Park offices of the Boston Consulting Group. Four years later, he was working for George Lucas at LucasFilms Ltd. There his job was to commercialize efforts spinning out of the company's Computer Division in Marin County, where the famous filmmaker set up shop after working for Francis Coppola's Zoetrope Studios in San Francisco (*American Graffiti* was partly filmed in San Rafael, Marin's largest city, and Lucasfilm's operations were headquartered there while construction had started on Skywalker Ranch in western Marin

County). The idea was to grow rich through the sale of cutting-edge digital technologies, but needing cash, Lucas ended up selling off big pieces of his computer division. Steve Jobs bought Pixar in 1986, while Bob Doris ran a different spin-off company called The Droid Works. That was sold and Bob and his wife, Mary Sauer, who also had worked at LucasFilm, along with some other Lucas "alumni" founded a digital sound and video editing company that went public in the 1990s and then sold for $800 million in 2010. The movies, it turned out, had been very good to the Doris/Sauer family. They were now running an angel fund they called Accanto Partners. We knew, as we pulled up to their offices in our rented car, the stakes could not have been higher.

"I've got a few degrees from Harvard," Bob told us as we settled in over coffee at his Tiburon office. It was hard not to be distracted by the view out his window—that is, if you consider the San Francisco Bay, Alcatraz, and the boats plying the waters under the Golden Gate distracting. "So I go and hang out at the Harvard iLab just for the heck of it when I'm in town. And frankly, I've found Boston is not a bad place to troll around for investment opportunities." Fine by us, we nodded, lined up on the sofa like prep school kids in for a lecture with the dean. Boston is smaller, he continued, and more the pace he wants for his lifestyle. "Out here is kind of overrun in a certain way, and Boston is more measured, and it's a little easier to access things," he said. We made small talk for a little longer and then he got down to business.

"You don't have a snowball's chance in hell of landing West Coast venture money," he told us, no matter how many meetings our HBS credentials won us. No self-respecting VC on Sand Hill Road was going to fund a company without a technologist attached to it, and a student project at that. Well, we thought. That was that.

Bob, who could pass as Steve Martin's younger brother, had the courtesy and decency to humor us as we ran through our pitch deck. But of course we already knew he was an ally, having seen the first iteration in Boston. He was sold on the company, he later told us, because of his own experience working in the consulting industry. Still, presenting to him was a great test run for our larger mission. One big fish was not going to be enough to sustain this dream. Watching our pitch, he later told us, "Whatever's in the business plan is usually proven wrong 10 minutes after you sign the check. You want a concept that makes sense, proof of a big enough market, a lack of competition, and things like that." The rest, he explained, is adaptability, as he learned himself helping George Lucas cash in on some of his more creative technological breakthroughs. Making a new market, he said, is always more challenging than exploiting one that already exists.

While he talked, we worked hard not to allow ourselves to get too distracted by the view out the window. The words "living the dream" came to mind. When the pitch was over and it was time for the rubber to meet the road, we laid it on the line. How much are you willing to invest?

Understand, for three young guys like us, this was like asking Dad for the keys to the car for a really important date. And we're talking about Dad's vintage roadster, not the family minivan. Fortunately, Bob must have seen something in us, because without blinking, he said a couple of hundred thousand dollars. You could have heard our gulps in Sausalito. But there was a catch. Of course there was a catch! We had to find a second person to invest alongside him. He didn't want to assume 100 percent of the risk. This was not as unsettling as it might seem. We still high-fived when we were out of earshot after we left his office. It just meant we now had to convince a second person to write a similarly large check. We had no idea who that investor might be. We had already exploited our networks to get this far, and our second-place finish back at HBS had not exactly garnered us a Rolodex full of HBS alumni on Sand Hill Road looking to fuel our dreams. But we were still ecstatic. No matter how many ways we imagined tripping ourselves up, here we were, breathing life into this thing.

The Silicon Valley VCs were right about one thing. We were not yet ripe for the picking. As we wended our way back to SFO and the long flight home, we knew that HourlyNerd was still a part-time project, no matter our full-time obsession. That summer, in keeping with our HBS alliances, Pat was working a summer job in Brussels, Rob was doing the same in Dallas, and Peter the same in Boston. The summer job is a big deal at HBS; the administration treasures its relationship with all those businesses around the globe that agree to hire students for a couple of months as junior associates. We could have reneged on our summer commitments and devoted ourselves full-time to the continued seeding of HourlyNerd, but that would have been academic, and most likely, career suicide. Tell a business you've changed your mind about working for them for the summer and rest assured, you will be remembered. And not in any way that you intended. What's more, the summer job helped us retain a hugely valuable asset, namely, our HBS email address. We did not have fat heads, and in fact, on more than one occasion, we had to downplay our Harvard lineage. On the other hand, that imprint and email address is one you always want to keep in your back pocket. As we would learn, you never know when it will come in handy.

So each of us individually spent the summer of 2013 doing the best we could to push HourlyNerd while trying not to mess up in our day jobs. By that point, we had expanded our ranks by one when a classmate from a different section, Joe Miller, volunteered to help us out. He had some background from running his family's small business and instinctively got what we were doing. Joe also came with some street cred. Prior to business school, he had worked at the fitness brand giant Equinox, where he had done the due diligence on the acquisition of SoulCycle, whose workout spaces are favored by the wealthy and the fabulous. Having Michelle Obama among their customers certainly didn't hurt business. Joe almost seemed more optimistic about our prospects than we did. Fresh blood is always a good thing.

We named Joe a cofounder and put him in charge of operations. He would also be responsible for looking into potential partnership deals. Making Joe part of our team meant one more thing for the West Coast VCs to snicker about when contemplating our small company. We had added a fourth person to our small company—another MBA with a summer job who couldn't commit to working fill time. Nothing like staffing up with a team of overworked millennials to show that fire in the belly.

We tried to stay in touch that summer through a weekly Sunday phone call. The time changed from week to week, so we all took turns being supremely inconvenienced across four times zones, stretching from Belgium to Colorado. Pat drew up a spreadsheet that tracked a to-do list broken into general categories: product development, fund-raising, sales, and marketing. Each of us took primary responsibility for at least one of those categories and agreed to play backup on the others. It all sounded good on paper, but mainly the calls were about keeping one another honest about our respective commitment to the company, despite being scattered across two continents. We dutifully took turns checking off bullet points on our HourlyNerd weekly to-do lists and then creating a new list for the following week. We were becoming quite adept at lists. Summer churned on.

Finding a second angel investor was a priority, of course. All the lists in the world were not going to put much-needed cash in our coffers. It was during one of our weekly calls that Joe had the brilliant idea of reaching out to Mark Cuban. Cuban had made his fortune in software in the early high-tech days and then added a splash of pizzazz to the mix by purchasing the Dallas Mavericks basketball franchise. He was a hands-on owner well known for prowling the courtside of his beloved team. Cuban's reputation only grew, and he became one of the stars of *Shark Tank*, the wildly popular reality show where normal guys like us pitched their business ideas to business sharks—angel investors who often critiqued you on national television for the privilege of getting a shot at early stage funding. Actually, Joe first proposed that we appear on *Shark Tank* as contestants, and meeting Cuban would be collateral, should we be so fortunate. But Rob the Realist shared the bad news that a *Shark Tank* win typically meant giving away as much as a 35 percent ownership stake in the company for just a few hundred thousand dollars. And even if none of the sharks chose to invest, the show's producers still often took a percent cut of the company.[1] "Well, that sucks," Joe announced. "Why don't we send an email directly to Cuban instead?" In addition to his Shark role, Cuban was an active and prominent angel investor with a net worth in the billions.[2] Why not write to him?

Preposterous ideas were becoming our bailiwick. Responsibility for this pie-in-the-sky idea fell to Rob. Finding Cuban's email proved surprisingly easy. It was listed right there on the website of AXS TV, the online television network he had created with Ryan Seacrest, the Creative Artists Agency, and CBS.

Our concept is pretty simple, Rob began in his pitch email. MBAs have spare time and business acumen and need money. Business owners are strapped for time and need business advice. We're here to match the two sides. In his handcrafted letter, Rob was sure to mention CNBC, *BusinessWeek*, and Bloomberg.

---

[1]You're the boss editors, June 2013: Is it worth a piece of your company to appear on Shark Tank? http://boss.blogs.nytimes.com/2013/06/12/is-it-worth-a-piece-of-your-company-to-appear-on-shark-tank/; http://jasoncochran.com/blog/8-things-you-didnt-know-about-shark-tank/.

[2]Kate Vinton, September 2016, Billionaire Mark Cuban Says He'll Give Trump $10 Million If He Agrees to an Interview with Cuban.

He even name-dropped CNBC and TheStreet superstar Jim Cramer's name, since he had once tweeted about our business. Obviously, we had no shame. We're in the midst of finalizing a $500,000 seed round, Rob continued, and would love to upgrade the quality of the advice and branding in the raise.

We heard back so fast that our first instinct was that we had been pranked. But in fact it was indeed Mark Cuban, and he had two questions. First, what's the valuation? (The higher the dollar value of a company, the smaller percentage of the company he would be purchasing in exchange for his investment.) Second: would you offer HourlyNerd as an on-demand service? (Imagine a kind of dial-a-nerd that allows you to log on to instantly engage with an expert whenever you needed one.)

Rob didn't hesitate when responding. Yes, we would offer an on-demand service, and our valuation was not that high. Cuban was now "Mark," and again he was quick to reply. "Okay, great," he responded. Only a few hours had passed since Rob had sent his initial email, yet we were already being handed off to a deputy who would take care of the details. It would be months before we actually met Mark Cuban or even spoke to him over a phone. The photo op could wait. We were in business!

Before we dreamt up The Cuban Option, we had initially thought of raising $250,000. But when Mark offered to pony up $450,000, we thought why not round off to a nice even number, so we bumped the overall round size to $500,000. Mark was asking to invest nearly that amount. We immediately got on the phone to our old pal, Bob Doris. He was thrilled that Mark Cuban was onboard. Cuban was a seasoned investor and a recognizable one to boot, who could give the company a real public relations bump. Doris suggested that we go for $750,000. Sure, why not? We felt like gamblers at a slot machine watching the coins pour out. Bob would invest several hundred thousand, Cuban was good for $450,000, and the remainder would come from friends and family.

We had started the summer recess thinking we were going for a measly quarter-mill. Two months later, that number had tripled to $750,000. Not bad, considering we were still working away at our summer jobs.

A few weeks later in a PR news release, Cuban announced he was investing in HourlyNerd because it "fills a need every entrepreneurial company faces." In that same statement, he said he expects his portfolio companies to be "heavy" users of the service.

The funny thing about an investment that size is that it doesn't quite seem real until you actually receive the money. We knew it was coming but didn't know exactly how or when. We took turns refreshing the HourlyNerd bank account literally every 30 minutes for four days. We kept seeing the same number over and over again: the $300 we had in the company coffers. Then one afternoon, when we checked for the umpteenth time, the wire had hit our account. We now had $450,300.

Peter took a screenshot and shared it with the team via email. We reveled in the moment, at least as much as you can revel staring at a pixilated screen that says you've hit pay dirt. Then reality set in. We had investors, both high caliber and tested, as well as family and friends. Now we had to go out and prove that they had not all made fools of themselves for believing in us.

CHAPTER **5**

The Talent Crunch

2014

We didn't really know what we were doing as far as sales. None of us did, including the founders. But we all were working for the same goal and that led us to be successful, even if early on it just felt frustrating.

—PAT KNEELAND, CATALANT EMPLOYEE #2

Try this on for size for a thought experiment. Tomorrow you take over as CEO of a Fortune 100 company we'll call the XYZ Corporation. The XYZ board of directors has chosen you specifically because you're an outsider. Shareholders complain that XYZ, a once-great company, has grown bloated and calcified. The business press mocks the company as an aging relic. You're the change agent brought in to transform the company whatever it takes—no matter how unpopular—even if it means closing down offices or jettisoning large quantities of employees. Your mandate is to reimagine XYZ for a new era.

Or, to take this exercise one step further, what if you could imagine XYZ as a blank slate, to be reconfigured as if a classroom full of MBA students instructed you to focus on the business side and not the social costs? Where would you begin?

We'll give it a shot. For starters, you probably keep many of the people. Companies need at least some full-time employees for continuity's sake, for institutional memory, to set and adjust a strategic vision. You might make changes in the C-suite or among the division heads and other managers, but you're not eliminating those positions, either. Let's surmise that XYZ is an industrial giant and needs full-time factory workers to populate its plants and stamp out the wide range of products it sells to businesses and consumers. The company still needs a complement of full-time support staff: receptionists, administrative assistants, mailroom workers, and such.

Now, what do you do about the rest of the enterprise? How about the comptroller's office, for example? You have to keep some full-time employees. But what about relying more on free agents brought in as each quarter demands, to work on your quarterly filings? Similar changes could be made in finance and accounting. In each case you'd want full-time people—for continuity, and because management requires a full-time devotion that does not come from a temporary employee. But think of the flexibility if there were a robust platform of people derived from the kind of operation we were building. We, of course, think about this day and night.

What about all the other departments populated by white-collar professionals? What if you need to devise a new marketing campaign? Or new advertising, a website, and social media? Enlisting outsiders means both a fresh perspective on your vision and continuous right-sizing of talent to economic need. It also could mean access to top-tier free agents who otherwise would be outside of XYZ's reach, contributing to your corporate mission. These are people who might never agree to uproot themselves to come work full-time for your company. Maybe they like where they live or have kids smack-dab in the middle of the formative years of their grade-school education. Or perhaps they prefer to remain independent because they have the skill set that allows them to do so. Mobility and technological know-how have made that ever so much more real. Skilled workers have extreme value, and yet they do not have to accept the golden handshake. But what if they'd be happy to take on a stimulating project that might require a trip or two to your headquarters, but otherwise allows them to work from wherever they like: home, the coffee shop, an Internet café during their travels through Croatia? How are you going to enlist this group?

Meanwhile, back in the marketing department at XYZ, it's time to execute on that new fall product plan and you're short of bodies. Do you start a hunt for three new marketing people, a couple of product experts, and a software person—or do you temporarily increase the department's head count by fishing in a talent pool like the one we're imagining? We suggest Plan B, because then you can easily ratchet down after the short-term need has receded, without the trauma and cost of layoffs. The project is completed, people are paid, and then they are free to do whatever they want until the next time XYZ needs their services. Bring in the right skills for the right projects at the right time and you are satisfying all your constituencies.

You can apply this same model to your sales department. You want people who devote their full attention to peddling the products that XYZ produces. But what about the talented salespeople who move on? They get a better offer, or need to move to be close to an aging parent, or just need a change of scene. Despite their successes—and the time and money the company has invested in them—they do leave. Why not employ a core staff of salespeople who express an interest to stay and grow and devote all their working hours to XYZ, along with their attendant leadership? Then supplement that loyal (and happy) core staff with those who might prefer to work part-time for you and yet still commit themselves to other things. In your downtime, they are not your worry. But when new products or demand calls for it, you can summon this temporary staff. The heavy hitters lead while the flexible workers pinch-hit. Not only does this cover your head count in busy times, but it is also a sensational recruiting tool. Draw people to your company on a project basis. And those who seem a good fit can—if the desire is mutual—be segued into a full-time posting.

In a time when the economy is calling for consistent fresh thinking and dynamic resourcing, from legal to communications to strategic planning, we are not advocating to offload people wholesale to make room for the new, free agent contingent. Institutional memory is important. So, too, is continuity and culture. But there needs to be an appreciation of a rebalanced workforce, as well, because workers are gravitating to this new lifestyle choice, and management is even less able to forecast the shape and size of its future needs. This is not a boutique concept. It is inevitable and it is coming fast.

Scaling back on your full-time staff load means a more nimble business, better able to react to new opportunities in real time. There is great advantage if XYZ can rapidly grow or shrink its head count depending on workload and deliverables. The platform we envision has the potential to give XYZ access to a far wider, deeper talent pool. Via online marketplaces, you will be able to find the technical people you need: the graphic designers and all those content kings and queens who have deep experience working strategy or brand management at corporate giants such as Procter & Gamble or Coke. Find the former SAP or Oracle salespeople who might help you find new customers in the enterprise. See if they'll bolt themselves to you for 6 or 12 months as your team aims to penetrate a new universe of potential buyers. If not, buy their time on a shorter-term basis for leads and sales training and supervising.

In this rejiggered world, we foresee the ability to travel light—and give yourself the leeway needed to survive the next wave of change. You will be rewarded, both for increased operating flexibility and innovative thinking. Think of it like this: As CEO, you have a set of problems to solve. The company, perhaps since its founding countless generation ago, has been locked into a dated hiring model. You're not going to bring back MS-DOS and dot matrix printing into your workspace. Why insist on perpetuating a labor model that technology is increasingly relegating to the dustbin? The old adage is that your most valuable asset is "human capital," but who says you have to stack it, file it, and pay for it in the same way? What if technology gave you a different way to craft your spend on human resources?

✿ ✿ ✿

There's a load of pain manifesting itself inside corporate America. The more due diligence we did to pursue our idea, the more obvious that became. As we built our business, the McKinsey Global Institute, the consultancy's well-regarded research arm, started asking big businesses about their troubles recruiting talent. They found that 4 in 10 companies in the United States—40 percent—were having a hard time filling open positions. The Boston Consulting Group warned that there was $10 trillion at risk because of what the third giant rounding out consulting's Big Three called "the global workforce crisis." Based on its research, McKinsey was predicting that 40 million people could benefit from the "flexible talent access" platforms being built by companies like ours. McKinsey found that these new marketplaces could generate up to $2.7 trillion in global economic impact—equal to the gross domestic product (GDP) of Great Britain. Maybe more relevant to the enterprise, McKinsey also estimated that they can improve a company's profit margin by up to 3 percent.

Another pain point is the high price of adding a new employee. The typical company spends as much as 150 percent of annual salary to locate, vet, and onboard a new management employee, according to the Institute for Research on Labor and Employment at the University of California–Berkeley.[1] Even if it were half that

---

[1]Andrei Hagiu and Rob Biederman, *The Dawning of the Age of Flex Labor*, September 4, 2015.

amount for other professional employees, spending 75 percent of an employee's annual salary is extremely expensive. There's also the cost to the bureaucracy of an approval process that can often take anywhere between three to six months inside a Fortune 1000 company and the sunk costs of training that employee before he even gets up to speed. In a word, adding head count is expensive.

And yet these days someone holding a job for three to five years seems a long time. Amazon and Google, for instance, or Mass Mutual and AFLAC, are among the companies where the median tenure for an employee hovers at around 12 or 13 months.[2] Therein lies the rub. The system is set up to keep employees for many, many years, and it is utterly cost ineffective to lose and then retrain one. Yet the culture is shouting out at us that people don't stay.

There is an added drag to this inefficient equation. Understaffed businesses regularly burn out existing employees by making them take up the slack. At what company do you hear cheers on a Friday afternoon when the manager announces that everyone is going to have to work all weekend because they don't have enough bodies to make a deadline?

The whole strategy seems self-defeating. Adding to an overworked employee's stress load only increases the chance that the employee might leave. And, of course, those most likely to find the exit doors are the ones with the talent to secure another job—precisely the people the company wants to keep.

There is a default option that large companies have traditionally turned to when they need a knowledge solution or professional services: the big consulting firms. These organizations are well known to be generalists with massive margins that charge around 10 times the rates they pay the consultants who actually work on the project. This kind of thinking may have kept Brooks Brothers

---

[2]http:// vivian giang, july 2013, a new report ranks america's biggest companies based on how quickly employees jump ship www.businessinsider.com/companies-ranked-by-turnover-rates-2013-7.

and Johnston-Murphy flush for many years in the 1970s and 1980s dressing the young and the eager in the uniform of the Street, but today that feels a dated solution to a modern-era problem. Electronic Recyclers, an innovative Fresno-based company that allows customers to dispose of digital devices in ways that are both environmentally responsible and safe, has been using HourlyNerd since 2013. Company CEO and cofounder John Shegerian had listened to pitches from the large consulting firms, but the prices were so high he demurred. John told *Inc.* magazine, "I have to dial 911 after I read them. Seriously, who wants to pay for that overhead? What Uber did to the black-car world, these guys at HourlyNerd are doing with the consulting world."[3]

It made us wonder: In a world where talent is king, what if business leaders were looking at the problem all wrong? What if the recruitment and retention problem was really one of access? At HourlyNerd, we felt management was making too great a distinction between "us" (the in-house employees) and "them" (the growing free agent workforce). We said, look at projects and deliverables instead of head count—and adjust the workforce accordingly, as if calibrating an engine. Clearly, the war for talent was on, but employers were not yet hearing the battle cry in the marketplace. It was becoming a simple truism that there is more talent outside company doors than in. Is this a trend managers could play catch-up on, or did they risk waking up to an office full of empty cubicles, with all their best talent defected to Starbucks, We Work, and every wired city park in America?

It was exciting to think that we were working on a solution to such a core problem for so many businesses. As we saw it, we were offering businesses a different way to organize themselves. Rather than dishing up whatever cosmetic rewards companies could offer

---

[3] Kimberly Weisul, April 2015, Need an MBA on the Cheap? Meet HourlyNerd, https://www.inc.com/kimberly-weisul/2015-30-under-30-hourlynerd.html.

to ensure people sit at their desk 50 weeks out of the year, what if business leaders focused instead on making work a place people wanted to be? Obviously for some employees, that was the case, and with the inducement of steady pay and some sense of stability, they could make up a business's core team. The rest of the head count needed a new way of thinking, however. Unhappiness was apparent—and rampant. Maybe their hang-up was geography or the commute—issues a business can't do much about. Maybe people heading for the doors (or wishing they could) saw the work they were doing as too narrow or confining. Work can be like food, and some folks really enjoy the all-you-can-eat buffet. Could a company keep employees happy if they had access to a wider body of creative and stimulating projects?

We understand that dropping out or going off grid was not the solution for many, or even most. But what if those who were looking for change and were willing to take a shot could find meaningful work through a platform like ours? We could provide the opportunity for the renegade worker and then help the businesses gain access to the very talent they so desperately needed. Workers still get paid and HQ gets vastly improved flexibility. Sure, it was a new way of thinking, but progress has shown no inclination to stand still. And with technology and mobility driving a generation that has never known anything but change, clearly something in the corporate wheelhouse was going to have to give.

❀ ❀ ❀

While we were confident we understood the market forces that were going to force management to course-correct, we still had to prove we could provide enough talent on the supply side to make ends meet. As we quickly learned, it wasn't only pain driving the other side of the equation. People weren't sure that if they walked out one door, another one would open up anytime soon. It used to be that independent work was largely the province of a few professions: writers, accountants, lawyers, graphic designers, and people with some pretty specific skill sets. But in 2002, Daniel Pink published his groundbreaking book, *Free Lance Nation* (subtitle: *The Future of Working for Yourself*). A decade later, LinkedIn cofounder Reid Hoffman published *The Start-Up of You*, which encouraged people to be more malleable in the way they looked at their career. Maybe that would mean working for a company for a few years, but it also might mean working as a free agent and selling your skills to the highest bidders.

An article published in the *Harvard Business Review* in 2012 documented the rise of the "super-temps"—a growing sector of people working for themselves because they could, not because they had to. More recently, a PricewaterhouseCoopers study found that nearly one-third—29 percent—of employees in China, Germany, India, the United Kingdom, and the United States wanted the chance to take much greater control of their work life: to work where they want and how they want.

In other words, people in the workforce were growing more comfortable working for themselves at the same time businesses were hunting for a new way to access talent. For the first time in at least a century, more humans seem to prefer work as free agents than as full-time staffers.

There are any number of explanations for this. One factor is the impact of the millennials descending on the workplace. This generation insists on getting more human satisfaction from work every day, and they are quick to seek alternatives when things aren't a good match. Technology is also playing a role. There is the stress of working in the 24/7 world. You need to love what you're doing given the constant demand of always being available. At the same time, technology points the way to freedom. Broadband is cheap and long-distance virtually free. Google Docs lets people work from home, at night, and on the weekends. Videoconferences happen all the time across time zones and cultures with coworkers who are calling in from every corner of the globe. Thursday night in New York is Friday morning in Asia. That means business is calling, and it knows no boundaries. Also, there is the new self-motivated marketplace known as eBay. Etsy. Self-publishing. Airbnb. And all the other creative and entrepreneurial opportunities afforded a generation that shudders at cubicle life and dreams of taking conference calls from the back of a motorbike in Phuket. Why should anyone stay with a company 50 hours a week for 30 years? It is a question we ask ourselves over and over again.

The bottom line is, a much wider range of specialty workers are drawn to the freelance life. But they still need to be fed, motivated, and inspired. There was a time in the 1950s and 1960s when the coolest people in the business world were the "whiz kids" of Ford, who introduced management controls and the discipline of metrics to today's corporation. Then came the Jack Welches and Jeff Immelts, who installed pillars of management theory interwoven throughout the workplace. Bill Gates and Steve Jobs took the stage and dominated it, followed by Jeff Bezos, Sergey Brin, Mark Zuckerberg, and the rest of the Unicorn generation. Much of this transformation was fed by the venture capitalists, who introduced a whole new class of zillionaires who had figured out their own way to write a ticket that looked nothing like the previous generations'.

Leadership in a black turtleneck and jeans became the Holy Grail, but to us, the king of the mountain these days is the intrepid freelancer.

Society doesn't make it easy on today's free agents. We speak of liberation for the working masses, but freedom, as famously put, indeed can just be another word for nothing left to lose. That is not how we envision it. The self-employed are a class that needs to be recognized, empowered, and, in our view, celebrated. As it stands now, if you go the indie route, you are going to pay both halves of Social Security rather than sharing the costs with your employer (from the official IRS site,[4] "if you're self-employed, you pay the combined employee and employer amount, which is a 12.4 percent Social Security tax on up to $118,500 of your net earnings and a 2.9 percent Medicare tax on your entire net earnings"). That equates to 15.3 percent of your annual wage, up to $118,500, or basically twice what a full-time employee would pay.

Even so, intrepid freelancers are striking out on their own, emboldened with the knowledge of their talents and their intrinsic worth on the open marketplace. They've also done the math—folks on our site tell us they make *more* on a per-hour basis than they did previously while full-time employed. Businesses are in a tough spot when their choices are adding to their head count or hiring one of the Big Three. The talented flexible worker has figured out he can work one-third fewer hours and make 50 percent more playing the arbitrage between the going rate for top-tier talent and the sunk costs of adding a full-time employee or hiring a consultant. There may be 200 reasons people prefer working for a corporation, including safety and security. Yet still hordes are venturing out to bushwhack their own way. Our culture rightfully celebrates the entrepreneur. And what are itinerant freelancers if not the ultimate entrepreneurs, absorbing 100 percent of the risk in seeing through their vision?

The pain point for these pioneers, before the marketplace era, was the uneven flow of work. There were few online outlets to help writers and lawyers seeking work. We found a few tiny folks trying to do something similar to what we were, but largely abroad. There was no market for the broader business community here in the States.

It is estimated there are somewhere around 29 million Americans working independently. We have no doubt there'd be

---

[4]https://www.ssa.gov/pubs/EN-05-10022.pdf.

many more if people knew they had convenient outlets like ours that can help generate demand opportunities. Demographers and economists have coined the phrase "alternative work" to describe those who have already joined this accelerating section of the job market (which includes freelancers and temp workers alike). Many were there by choice, but not all. For the countless others, who at their very core knew they wanted to be unshackled, they would need help finding work in a more efficient manner. Craigslist made sure there would be no more classifieds in the back of the local newspaper and a red pen to circle the jobs. Randomly knocking on the doors of the country's 29 million–plus businesses also seemed a daunting task.

It was exciting to know that our marketplace for high-end talent was a potential solution. The demand was there; the key would be to help the two sides find one another. The Nerds were finding us without much effort on our account. If we could attract enough work to our site, we could help freelancers of all types smooth out the inherent lumpiness of their month-to-month work life. It was a true scratch-our-heads moment. What had we stumbled on? Was this a niche market that we'd tap out in six months or a year, or did we have a chance to be the eBay of human capital, except it was heads, not used baseball cards for sale?

CHAPTER 6

The Match Game

Winter–Spring 2014

The opportunities for work on the Catalant platform are phenomenal. Every day there are easily a dozen new projects posted and they run the gamut: market research projects, financial projections, data analysis, and marketing, serious corporate strategy work. All kinds of intellectually challenging and rewarding projects.

—KARA YOKLEY, A STRATEGY AND DATA ANALYST FROM CHICAGO

Not long after announcing our Seed round in September 2013, we were hunted down by Dan Nova, an HBS class of 1991 graduate and veteran venture capital investor in Boston. Though we had just raised more money than we knew what to do with, Dan and his partners at Highland Capital were excited to get involved. Though we had grown slightly since the humble first-year days prowling Harvard Square and its micro-businesses, the company was still quite raw. The Highland folks, however, saw something special in the opportunity. We were flattered (if surprised) by their interest and quickly closed a few million dollars of additional funding, with Greylock Partners joining in the round as well. All of a sudden, we were a real, VC-backed company!

With money in the till and a breeze in our sails, our focus was also beginning to change. The original idea for HourlyNerd had been predicated on harnessing the time of less-experienced MBAs who'd be happy to pick up an extra 50 bucks an hour helping out small businesses with interesting projects. Initially, a prospective expert couldn't sign up and start bidding for the assignment without an email address from a respectable business school or affiliated alumni association. But as it turns out—and one could argue we should have known—most MBA students didn't have that much extra time on their hands. Larger companies also wanted to see more experienced folks working on the more sophisticated opportunities. And now that we were off campus and back in the real world, we were going to have to broaden our view of the prototypical expert.

One interesting fact we had uncovered during our time on the street supported our theory about disruption in consulting. Turnover among the Big Three was astronomical. For a host of reasons—burnout, stress, reevaluation of life goals—people did not stay. This had to mean opportunity for us. Where did these people go? What were they doing with their stalled or transformed careers? And could we find them, tap into them, and put them to work?

Typically, working for a consulting firm of any size involves long hours and extensive travel. This surely had to be a factor in the churn, as well. What about reaching out to new parents who had the requisite skills to perform at the highest level still but wanted to remain closer to home and work less? We saw in the changing environment of more flexible parenting there was an able-bodied force of stay-at-home parents who had opted for time with their newborns but still wanted to stay relevant in the workplace. These considerations reflected exactly what we knew: times were changing and talented people were in the market for interesting new solutions to meet their desire to work in a different way.

Another factor that was causing people to drop out was the aging demographic of millennials—and their parents! One of the most common topics of conversation among friends and colleagues was the care of their elderly parents. If you lived in the same town as your folks, this might mean cutting back on your backbreaking hours to schlep out to a childhood home or a care facility to be the good kid. If your mother or father had relocated to Arizona and you were putting in 60-hour weeks in Manhattan, well, you had a problem. And we had the solution. The flexible worker can be in two places at one time. And if one of those places requires you to uproot and be there for a loved one, there is no reason you can't still earn a living performing the high-level work you were doing in a more urban setting.

Yet another factor fomenting this change in attitude was that the workforce was becoming more and more responsive to the careers of two breadwinners. The notion that one person's job was more important than the other's was becoming a dated relic. So what happens if one spouse's job opportunity precipitates a geographical career move? Didn't that leave the other talented half of a couple hunting for new employ? It is a dialogue that is becoming more and more common, and we believed that HourlyNerd could become the third spoke in the wheel. If spouse A has been offered the big in-house legal job in Denver, Spouse B does not have to stay behind for six months while conducting a job hunt. He can pick up and share the U-Haul drive across America, all the while bringing in temporary, on-demand assignments. Who knows—spouse B might ultimately decide that this flexibility thing is a boon to their lifestyle and landing that full-time gig can wait. We were not beyond believing that our platform had the ability to seriously change some minds and lives.

For all these reasons—and countless others that we were hearing all the time in our travels—it was becoming evident that a highly talented workforce was seeking a new way to work, they were not sure how to find it, and they were worried about potentially getting left out in the cold. It all made perfect sense to us. You could quantify it. And we did. HourlyNerd had the numbers to provide companies with talent, and talent with access to the types of work they would otherwise never get unless they were gainfully employed in the old system. The match concept was taking off. As one eager respondent said to Pat, "Holy hell, I can do a project for a company the caliber of GE and still stay solo and operate my own shop? Where do I sign up?" We knew that HourlyNerd had the kind of stuff this newly displaced talent pool could never otherwise get on their own. And they were, happily for us, responding in droves.

Beyond the good daily news, we were seeing the wider trends pointing to exactly what we guessed just a couple of years ago when we dreamed this up. The freelance economy was going to happen one way or the other. People were realizing that quality of life mattered as much, if not more, than the security of a regular paycheck. The constrictions that had kept the previous generation locked in place at a desk were dropping away. Meanwhile, the change was starting to happen on the demand side, and the demand side, we realized, was serving as an enabler for the supply side. The momentum we were observing was just a little staggering.

It was our belief that anyone who really wanted more flexibility in their life—and boasted deep and impressive resumes—could afford to venture out on their own if they were willing to make the leap. What we knew—and they might not yet—was that their expertise was a masked and potent asset, waiting to be unleashed to a business marketplace hungry for talent. Business needed people like this unaffiliated talent pool, and they would pay for it. MBAs, PhDs, veterans of the Big Three consulting firms, even students who were still enrolled in graduate school and recent graduates—all had cachet and power, if only they knew where to sell it. It was on us to start pushing this idea out to the world that we had access to a wider, more experienced pool of experts. If we could build momentum around the idea that this group existed and we had harnessed them, then we could potentially attract a larger universe of businesses—the demand side—and that in turn would allow us to garner the higher rates for a higher caliber of expert. It was a virtuous cycle that could raise the rates for our experts and amp up our business model by helping to boost our own revenues.

* * *

While our expert pool was expanding, our view of the target customer was also changing. At the outset, we were happy to host a work request from any business, no matter the size. Keep in mind our first client was a veggie burrito hut. We were humble beyond belief. That was reflected in the size of the average project posted on our site: $2,000 at the start of 2014. But we were also realistic. Beans and cheese were probably not going to fuel the future of our expansion plan. With that in mind, we were attempting to build new relationships with some pretty heavy hitters. We still viewed the small business owner as our primary customer, but we had no hesitation about fishing in much deeper waters. The problem was that we weren't sure what we were going to find out there. We'd scored some C-suite-level meetings and senior management sit-downs, but more than once we had been greeted with blank stares. Were we selling a product, or a service, or an entire change in thinking? Change management and organizational shift are some pretty weighty topics when you have five minutes and a watery cup of coffee to make your point. What's more, not everyone warms to your presence when you tell them they are living in the past. "Say, your organization is wallowing in its own inertial quicksand. Can we help?" We were getting very good at finding the door out on our own.

Still, we believed in the platform and we knew how to talk the talk. It was walking the walk where our learning curve had a long way to go. Translation? Listening was a skill we were getting very good at. We had no choice. We had a new business model with a new class of worker and we had little precedent on which to structure our pitch. How could we sell the customers if we didn't know what they wanted or needed? It was time to get aggressive. So we pressed our button-down shirts, donned our blazers, crossed our legs, and let the customers tell us what they needed. We empowered our ragtag early sales team to listen more than speak and learn about what the customers cared about and how we should talk about our product and what that product needed to do.

The advantage to our scattershot sales approach was that we were accumulating knowledge at a breakneck clip. We'd find ourselves talking in the morning to a small retail business with a few hundred thousand dollars in revenues, and then in the afternoon we might be sitting down with a manager in command of a hundred million dollars a year in sales. Both of these potential customers were huge sources of valuable learning for us. Because we had started out small, we felt we had a pretty good sense of touch and compassion from the mom-and-pop concerns. They knew what their pain points were and had no problem describing them, and we had no problem helping provide them with the talent to go out and fix things.

However, we discovered that the larger enterprises were having their own unique set of troubles retaining or finding access to talent. We asked everyone we met, from HR managers to CEOs, how they felt they were doing in employee engagement. Clearly, it was a loaded question. More often than not they repeatedly threw up their hands in frustration. They'd tried everything and nothing worked. That was good news for us. We felt we had the solution they were looking for, and we had a way to put it to work for them that trumped the old consulting model.

One of our early wins was an industrial giant that was bleeding money on a fluctuating cycle and actually saw the logic to what we had to offer. This company had a seasoned marketing team that was more than adept at doing their job. They were very service- and ticket-oriented and reactive to market needs. The problem was those needs were extremely volatile and unpredictable from month to month and quarter to quarter. One month the whole department would be maxed out at 120 percent producing volumi- nous amounts of material, and then the next the demands dropped precipitously and they were running at 60 percent optimization at best. They were trapped committing to a spend on full-time employees who were intermittently working until their eyes bled, followed by fallow times when half the staff was checking Facebook or watching World Cup soccer from their cubicle on their phones. Not the best use of people power for sure.

The long-term solution we all came up with involved this company maintaining the department with a baseline crew of around 70 percent on staff and then supplementing the power surges with Catalant. They were able to correct for the fluctuations—the unpredictable spikes and dips—with the on-demand team they retained from us. So they got the best of all worlds. They did not have to make a drastic transition from W-2s and full-time employees to a totally on-demand 1099 team. They swung the pendulum halfway and kept an experienced team that had plenty of institutional knowledge and could handle the baseline workload. Then when things peaked, they could quickly engage our experts—along with their fresh eyes and fresh focus— for the one-off projects that did not merit having a half-dozen staffers sitting around twiddling their thumbs for the percentage of time that the workload did not merit. We saw it as a win for all sides.

* * *

In fact, there was a big strategic manpower shift going on at the larger companies, and we were darned pleased to be sitting in the on-deck circle getting our swings. The most demanding skill sets employers needed were not coming from McKinsey and Bain anymore; they were coming from the tech companies and broader innovation economy. This is where the innovation and agility and creative thinking were getting birthed. What's more, the structure of the large consulting firms no longer created value the way it used to back in the 1980s. The lumbering team structure of a typical consulting gig had grown dated and mossy. Hiring a consulting firm would all but ensure that truly innovative, off-the-wall ideas would ever make it into presentations. You'd get spreadsheets and PowerPoints and more wasted time in meetings than you ever bargained for. You'd also get a ticking clock on every manager's desk known as billable hours. But at the end of the day, were you getting state-of-the-art thinking and solutions? Not so much so, we believed. And we had an inkling others were starting to agree.

So we knew we were selling a system that could slice through the traditional factors that make large-scale consulting firms ineffective, while also bringing companies an intriguing and hungry new set of brains—and those brains rested on the shoulders and bodies of men and women who would never be caught dead working in a consulting shop. We felt we were appealing on many levels to the companies that most valued fresh ideas and fresh blood, for lack of a better term. That was our sweet spot. Which is not to say that consulting was dead. We understood that there would be a role for consulting for the largest multiyear, multidisciplinary projects. Boards and management will still surely cling to the consulting ways. But it was our belief that way too much consulting muscle was being brought in and wasted on projects that could be satisfied with on-demand expertise. Especially where you have companies using a McKinsey or Bain for gross staffing needs. For our nickel, that was like shooting a mosquito with a bazooka. Where is the value in hiring a Big Three firm to manage a hospital gig for six months? The business logic for that is far too much of a stretch when there are alternatives. It may have worked for the last

40 years because the on-demand flexible workforce consisted of a different constituency with a different set of skills. But HourlyNerd had created a supply side rich with expertise that cast a light on the diminishing returns for much of the work that had once been relegated to consulting.

Would the enterprise get it, though? They had to if our theory was going to prove out, and we believed we were on the right track. Change was happening fast, and being behind the curve was sure to be a costly, if not lethal mistake for most or many businesses. The talent disruption that we were sparking was the place for smart management to lead, get ahead of the inflection point, and enjoy a truly differentiated advantage as the employer of choice in a flexible worker economy. That was the gap we hoped to fill. But getting the message through and getting someone to act on it was no small feat. If anything, the bigger the business, the deeper their existential crisis. They weren't supposed to be having a talent problem, and yet their woes were draining their resources. The challenge was how to convince these bigger, slow-moving companies that their view of the workplace was becoming dated, and this tiny little start-up in Boston was sitting on the answer to a new way of doing work.

CHAPTER 7

The Flexible Workforce

It was on my first day of work that I realized I had walked into a company in the primordial stage of existence—a company still struggling to make sense of the world.

—RICH GARDNER, HEAD OF SALES, CATALANT (NÉE HOURLYNERD)

Many have dreamed for a long time of a work life that meant more than a daily commute to a job they didn't particularly like. But before the Internet and before remote collaboration tools, most felt like their choices were limited. They suffered through the 9 to 5 and lived for the weekends—and the precious few weeks of vacation they were afforded each year. For the brave and the few, when the pressure became too much, they threw themselves into the job market and more often than not ended up in another dead-end job that simply shifted the pervasive sense of dissatisfaction from one company to another: another soul-deadening commute, another job description, perhaps even another town. It did not take long to see that the work/life balance problem was more pervasive than we knew. Or as David Byrne of the Talking Heads put it: "Same as it ever was. Same as it ever was."

Prior to the advent of mobile technology, the freelance life, at least by reputation, seemed mostly limited to the creative classes. Going out on your own came with an implicit understanding that you were different in some way: an artist, a writer, a musician.

Freelance did not apply to the mass of men and women—those living the fabled life of quiet desperation. However, as technology became pervasive, the balance started to shift, and that was the cue we picked up on when we brainstormed our HourlyNerd concept to life. There were more opportunities, more of an acceptance of a change in attitude, and, as we were learning, a growing share of the population who were willing to consider the risk of a life of free agency.

This was a unique bunch, trailblazers if you will, who trusted in their abilities enough to tap into their networks—or look for new ones—in search of meaningful work. Take Anshul Agrawal, whom we met through HourlyNerd in the fall of 2013. Anshul had earned his MBA at the University of North Carolina's Kenan-Flagler Business School and then put in two years as director of engagement at a New York–based company called Next Jump, before deciding the mainstream course was not for him. He took the leap to venture off on his own in 2012. Newly free, Anshul returned to his hometown of Toronto and decided to specialize in market research projects in the consumer packaged goods (CPG) space. He got busy on our platform, bidding on something like 50 jobs before finally securing his first project. It proved to be an auspicious beginning.

One advantage of our site is that we maintain a detailed ratings system for every project a Nerd encounters. Succeed at a task and the system kicks in and leads to goodness for all involved. In Anshul's case, he thrived at his first assignment and got the scores to prove it. He quickly won his next project, then another, and then what morphed into a steady stream of business after that. To date, he has completed more than 100 projects through the site. In fact, Anshul's success within the system was so good that to keep up with demand, he had to hire others to farm out the overflow of work coming his way. From working as an exploratory freelancer, Anshul turned his one-man consultancy into a boutique consulting firm. Now, on his LinkedIn page, he lists market leaders in the beverages, software and consumer industries as companies he has helped explore potential growth opportunities.

Anshul was a storybook success tale for our business. Not only had he broken free from the shackles of a steady, go-nowhere job, but he successfully crafted a work/life schedule more to his liking. Since signing on with HourlyNerd, he has been able to pay off his business school loans and take his wife on their first-ever vacation. We sensed he would not be looking back anytime soon.

We were high-fiving in the office about Anshul's fantastic trajectory, yet in the same breath it illustrated the challenges laid out before us. We were rapidly accumulating talented people like Anshul, but we had to fortify the demand end of our business with a much larger pool of companies willing to test out our site. This did not simply mean knocking on more doors. We had tried that already, and after making introductions at about 300 places of business, we had a whopping total of five customers to show for our efforts. This was not a model that was going to bear fruit in the short term. We had to make a case to the wider marketplace that HourlyNerd was not just a matchmaker but a whole new way of doing business.

Disruption in the workplace has been rightly identified as a digital revolution, nearly since the advent of the first clunky desktop computer. Famously, Moore's law came about in the early 1970s, suggesting that computer speed was going to double every two years. This concept was quickly adopted by the burgeoning IT industry and then spread like an inkblot in the turbulent waters of the changing workplace. In a word, everything was changing, and it was going to continue to as processing power, then mobility, amplified. Everything we see—and that the new workforce experiences today—is the direct result of the speed of change. But while the focus has been on the explosive growth of technology, it has taken infinitely longer for the social changes it brought about to catch up to the worker and employer and grab a foothold in the lexicon of work. Essentially, we created a workforce that could run at 150 miles per hour, but we left the talented experts on a track designed for 60 per at best. These men and women could adapt and do the job and do it well—but companies were many miles behind at adapting and figuring it out. Our idea was on a collision course with reality. What if we created a flexible workforce with nowhere to go? That could only spell big trouble down the road.

We'd heard from top managers that they were having trouble finding the right people for the right jobs, and yet we were not having the success we anticipated—and needed—to sign them up. What we were learning on the fly was that the only way we were going to get these companies to consider change was to shine a light on their pain. We asked them over and over again: Do you know where the skills and competencies in your company lie? And over and over we heard the same misinformed answers: "Technology, innovation, collaboration. That's what we're good at." We respect-fully disagreed. These were paradigms, not people. You can't walk into someone's office and say, "Hey, we need some innovation on the 24th floor. Can you send some up?" People have to be attached to tasks and deliverables, and that's where companies were coming up short. And the numbers bore it out.

We asked our contacts at one large client the same question—Where are your core competencies in your workforce?—and they laughed. They said they had no idea! A double-barreled no: they did not know the talent they had inside the company and they did not know how to find it. What this underscored for us was that large companies were unlikely to thrive and succeed in the long term unless they came to the realization that they were not tooling up for the future. If they were planning to rely on a full-time workforce and they couldn't even identify their talent pool, how would they retain their most valuable asset?

Marisa Goldenberg signed up at our site in the fall of 2014. She had earned a degree in computer science from Princeton and an MBA from Harvard. She had started her career in enterprise software start-ups, but after the dot-com boom and bust of the late 1990s, she joined Dell as a corporate strategy consultant, working in the office of chairman Michael Dell. By the time she left the company in 2009, she was director of its global business operations. Marisa knew the ins and outs of the company that employed her, but did *they* know anything about their employee at all? Marisa describes herself as an "extreme introvert" who still managed to thrive in the workplace. But as an introvert, the constant noise and interruptions in a cubicle environment often sapped her energy during the day. "I had always received top performance ratings, despite not operating at my full potential," she said, which left her wondering, "How much had I left on the table?"[1] (Dell has of late become a true pioneer in the flexible workforce, with a 2020 goal of a 50% remote workforce.)[2]

After leaving her large corporate role behind, Marisa explored several start-up ideas of her own. She picked up consulting projects on the side through her own personal network, and upon discovering HourlyNerd was intrigued by the business model and the potential to greatly expand her business. Marisa quickly proved herself on the platform, and soon was winning large enterprise projects with C-level stakeholders at Fortune 50 companies. She could deliver tremendous impact for clients while working remotely with just a phone and an internet connection. As her business grew, Marisa recruited a partner and a bench of consultants who were happy to collaborate remotely on project work. The on-demand industry had lit a spark in Marisa, which

---

[1] Marisa Goldenberg, April 2016, A Place in the Business World Where Women, Minorities and Introverts Can Thrive https://www.linkedin.com/pulse/place-business-world-where-women-minorities-can-marisa-goldenberg.

[2] http://money.cnn.com/2016/06/09/pf/dell-work-from-home/index.html.

was "fueled by the positive externalities" she found—including enhanced productivity. "The remote setting allowed me to conserve my energy rather than drain it in the overload of stimulation from a traditional office," she wrote. "I am more productive and higher performing than I've ever been. Which makes me wonder—how much productivity do companies lose when their introverted employees don't work in their ideal environments?"[3]

The traditional workforce's loss was Marisa's gain. But that was a message that needed to travel far beyond most company's walls. We got it. It was practically our raison d'être. We existed solely to custom-tailor jobs that suited people at companies that needed help. But if those companies did not see this, our growth was going to become extremely limited in very short order.

Our founding team existed on an interesting plane when it came to crafting strategy, putting out fires, or both! While Pat was viscerally, emotionally moved by the challenge of helping people liberate themselves from the tyranny of work, Rob had a tendency to think more philosophically; he was as much a hard-charging entrepreneur as a would-be economics professor. The two approaches worked well together when it came to shifting corporations as much as minds.

"There is a market elegance to our proposition," Rob explained. "The existing system, as it is structured, does not create as much employment as it should. And it creates needless shocks to the system and volatility, because when demand falls 10 percent, the unfortunate existing answer is to lay off 10 percent of your workforce."

Rob reflected that today's employers were operating in the dark on a system that had gelled decades ago during the manufacturing and production boom. "If you were a traditional CPG company,"

---

[3]https://www.linkedin.com/pulse/place-business-world-where-women-minorities-can-marisa-goldenberg.

he said, "the mission of your company did not change that much. You got good at manufacturing and you got good at marketing and you were good at distributing cereal. The way to win was getting slightly better at that." Companies, he said, were still operating on that 1950s premise in a twenty-first-century economy. "The existing system did not set us up for radical innovation because back then people got trained to do something really well, about 2 to 4 percent better each year. If there was radical thinking, it typically was coming from outside your organization." Therein lies the problem, he said.

If companies were still operating under the yoke of dated thinking, the new breed of employee most assuredly was not. Kara Yokley was seeking flexibility when she discovered HourlyNerd in 2014.[4] Like so many of our Nerds, Kara had the kind of blow-away resume we knew would impress potential clients. She had gone to Harvard undergrad, where she studied applied math and economics, and then managed a group of global researchers studying the high end of the hardware market (Silicon Graphics, Cray, Sun Microsystems, IBM). She'd earned her MBA at Wharton and then went to work for J.P. Morgan. Even with that kind of enviable, blue-chip pedigree, apparently she was looking for more, because she would learn about us while reading a blog post talking about nontraditional paths of work. She checked out the platform and felt heartened, Kara told us, because she came across so many projects that aligned with her skill sets. If only her employers knew that she was not scoping the competition, but rather, a different lifestyle altogether, they might have been able to retain a top talent.

"I always knew that I wanted to have a life that provided flexibility to explore the world," Kara said. "I had the sense that it would be difficult to do that in a traditional corporate job. And

---

[4]https://www.linkedin.com/in/kara-yokley-2a471a25/.

so it made sense to align work and some of my private passions as well." Kara, based in Chicago, would take on a wide range of projects she located through our site, including one for a company exploring alternative directions for its business. "The work I did informed the board," she said. "It was gratifying to know that my research and presentation would be helpful in guiding their discussions for the strategic direction of the company." Kara was having the kind of work experience and impact she had dreamed about but that seemed so elusive to her—and to so many trapped within the corporate world. And that corporate world, we knew, was operating at a knowledge deficit.

If we were going to capture the larger marketplace, we were going to have to pinpoint for management the very pain points they seemed to be missing. And this meant, at the most foundational level, we had to illuminate how work had changed. From an HR standpoint, the hunt for talent was still an analogue process. They had a job that needed filling, or perhaps it was a "role" or responsibility that existed on some dated flowchart. If they could not fill it with the existing head count, they would run an ad, or put the ask out to an agency that then ran an exhaustive and expensive search for the talent to fill that position. This was not only costly, but it was a way of thinking that refused to adapt to the changing times.

What companies needed—and we knew existed—was a whole new mind-set with which to view their workplace. Instead of playing to the role, why not play to the deliverable? To put it in the vernacular of breakfast cereal, you could hire or fire as the demand for cornflakes rose and shrank—or you could change your strategy in such a manner that it allowed for a whole new way of thinking about breakfast cereal. New products, new markets, and a whole new way of defining your business created agility. Technology-based industries had gotten that message from the git-go. Think back to the golden age of the Internet start-up. Was Amazon just about books any longer? Facebook simply a place to connect with college classmates? And perhaps most ubiquitously, look at Google. A dozen years ago we had barely come to terms with the word "search" as a business. How could anyone possibly monetize that?

Technology may have led the way, but now it was clear to us that it was time for the rest of the business world to catch up. And that means a wholesale change in thinking about how they view their internal workforce. Naturally, we don't expect the corporate structure that has existed for decades to fold up and die. But "outside-in" thinking is going to prevail, and that means the leaders will have to look at, feel, and touch their workplace differently. They will have to become flexible in their grander scale of thinking if they hope to keep up and more so, take advantage of the strategic opportunities that agility provides. And if they don't see the writing on the wall, their workers are going to spell it out for them. If this seems obvious to us, it's not because we took better notes at B-school. The growth of HourlyNerd was shouting out the message loud and clear. We want change, our workers were saying, and if we can't find it at the office, we'll find someone or some way to locate it ourselves.

Anshul had gone from a dead-end job to running his own Toronto boutique. Marisa had expanded her client reach and impact, and enabled her team to collaborate in ways that maximized energy and productivity. And it's no surprise, given Kara's background, that she's been so successful on our platform as well. In many ways, Kara exemplifies the change we foresee best. She became so busy that she brought on someone to help her with the workload. Soon after, she brought on four other like-minded consultants to join her team. She and her husband had their first child and like any new parents found their life turned upside down. But instead of massive life and job upheaval, they were able to adapt and change their work to fit the lifestyle they had chosen—not the other way around. That hit all the right marks for Pat's deeply felt position on work/life balance and, in the same breath, captured Rob and Peter's belief in the inevitable changing economic equation.

"With the Catalant (formerly HourlyNerd) platform, clients are most concerned about your capabilities, and your ability to deliver the product that they require," Kara told us. "Our family could be in Taiwan or Costa Rica and I would still be able to do interesting, fulfilling work without compromising on lifestyle. A platform like Catalant (formerly HourlyNerd) really gives me the flexibility to do that."

Experts like these had sent a strong message that we were on the right track. Now the only question was, would corporations hear the same message and follow suit?

CHAPTER 8

Disruption

Summer–Fall 2014

Companies of all sizes should be tapping into the global brain.

—Mark Cuban

Ben Zlotoff had seen himself as a lifelong "Bainie." He had worked there as an associate prior to going to Harvard for business school and absolutely loved it. "I drank the Kool-Aid," he would tell us. He had studied mechanical engineering in college and was eager to find a way to put his quantitative skills to use in the business world. Going to work as a junior consultant at Bain & Company seemed the perfect way to meld the two. He loved the people and apparently the feeling was mutual. They provided a steady drip of promotions, training, and increasing leadership opportunities. Ben didn't hesitate when after two years at the firm, Bain & Co. offered him a deal similar to the one Bain Capital had offered Rob: free tuition with a promise to come back after earning his MBA. "I thought I wanted to be a Bain partner," Ben said. "That was my life plan."

He was a few months from graduating HBS when the disconcerting thoughts started to rattle around his brain; the idle, troubling sense that maybe something was askew. He already knew he was on a steady and largely predictable path, where he wouldn't be breaking much new trail. Was this really his dream, he wondered?

It was that rumbling sense of curiosity that prompted Ben to visit us at our two-room Bromfield Street office. We were all the same year at HBS, but in a different section. We knew Ben vaguely; we had run into him around campus and competed against him in intramural sports. Ben was in a class with Rob during our final semester when, as Ben tells the story, he began to compare his own post-graduation path to those of some of his other classmates. "I was feeling pretty pleased with myself about my plans," he said. "That was until I got to know Rob and got a whiff of what the HourlyNerd team was up to." All of a sudden, as Ben recollects, the straight and narrow began to look a little too straight and way too narrow. He put it to us this way: "I had this visceral feeling of envy. What you guys were doing seemed more personally authentic, more special, and more fleeting an opportunity than what I was about to pursue."

Ben wasn't scheduled to start at Bain until September. He urged Rob to let him come to HourlyNerd to hang out over the summer. "I decided to give the start-up thing a chance," Ben recalled, "just so I could be a part of it, even for a couple of months." He joined us in June of 2014, starting as an intern, bringing our ranks up to around a dozen.

"I had more fun during my first week at HourlyNerd than I'd had on many of my favorite consulting projects," Ben said. He closed his first sale on his fourth day on the job. That's when he knew he might be facing a hard decision. "In traditional consulting, the highs for me as a junior associate were typically intellectual. 'Cracking the case'—consulting speak for uncovering a project's breakthrough insight—was satisfying and fun. Helping advise a client and seeing them succeed felt good. I'm forever grateful for what Bain gave me, most especially the world-class training and a loyal network of peers and mentors. But ultimately, I found myself craving the professional satisfaction of being a builder and operator, not an advisor. After that first sale, I mashed my hand five times on our 'sales bell' for having helped launch a five-thousand dollar project. Hooting and hollering, high fives and an endorphin rush ensued. At that moment, I knew that I was addicted to building this business."

It was not long after Ben started that we landed phone time with a potential senior enterprise client, which was very rare for us in those days. As big as our aspirations were, we were still aware of our humble veggie burrito roots. No one in the company outside of Pat had any consulting experience, and so we convinced Ben to join us on the call so we could say, "On the phone is Ben, who worked at Bain." Shameless? You bet. But we took advantage of every asset we had.

We were onto a potentially big deal and it was incumbent on us to make it sound like we knew a lot more about the consulting world than we did. The only problem putting Ben on the call was that he was still just an intern. So right before the call began, the brain trust huddled and made a management decision. We called Ben in. "Congratulations. You're now our head of client strategy." We didn't have time to see if he'd accept. We dialed up the client. Ben would be our resident "scoping" expert—the person tasked with sussing out the dimensions of a project for any particular business that fell under his bailiwick, and then helping us figure out pricing and other considerations. This was critical to our thinking. How much might a project cost, and how would a business even think about sizing up an assignment with us? What about timing—start dates, deadlines, and such? Spelling out the deliverables and any of another dozen concerns a customer might have was a critical piece of the equation, and we needed Ben as much as he wanted us. This was staffing by desperation, but thanks to Ben's business acumen and passion for the gig, we were in business. Whenever we were lucky enough to get a prospective enterprise-sized client on the phone, it would be Ben's role to help them think through this stuff on the fly. "We're not growing fast enough," a prospective customer might say—and it was on Ben to break that down into an actual set of tasks that could be quantified and bid out.

Ben turned out to have a knack for locating other pain points as well, as we tried to understand the needs of the larger customer. Traditionally, when a company invites an outside consultant into an enterprise, there is a call for a nondisclosure agreement (NDA) and often, a complex legal contract. With Ben's experience at Bain, we figured we could rely on him to help us figure out those technical details, because we were running into them again and again with the large clients we wanted to bring in. We had underestimated the challenge of scaling up our billables. It couldn't be 10 times harder to convince a business to post a $40,000 job as one at $4,000, could it? We were rather simplistically—and optimistically—looking to the bottom line, without a sufficient amount of evidence to the contrary. No one could accuse us of overthinking things in our early days. We were glad to have Ben. He proved to be a valuable asset.

As it turned out, cutting these deals can be far more complicated than we'd ever imagined. We'd get the lead and put Ben on the phone with the rest of us and we'd hop off feeling amped and ready to pop the champagne. Then there'd be meetings and more meetings, followed by delays that baffled and frustrated us. Presumably higher-ups or maybe someone in the comptroller's office was weighing in on what we were proposing. There were considerations around intellectual property, compliance, and confidentiality. Everything was more complicated as we continued to "climb out of the basement," as HBS's Dina Wang had memorably put it.

There was also the trust issue. It was one thing to get a small business to commit a few hundred, or even a few thousand dollars, to allow our experts to get them out of a jam. However, once we started dealing with larger companies, it was a whole different ball game. We saw it as akin to Amazon's growing pains in the

1990s, when they went from asking people to buy a $12 book to getting them to commit to a $200 pair of shoes and a microwave oven in one click. There was definitely a leap of faith.

In the universe we were creating, the business that was thinking about posting a $40,000 job listing on our site had a lot of worries. What about that NDA? And at the most basic level, what if, for that amount of money, a consultant did shoddy work? We were selling a dating website for business. The two parties—the hiring firm and our consulting Nerd—would probably never meet face to face. They might not engage in more than a single phone conversation before consummating a deal. And all they had was our word and the stamp of approval we gave a consultant whom we didn't really know much about, plus our assurance that should anything go wrong, we'd fix it. We believed in the system. But we needed a lot more large enterprise businesses to back us up and prove our point.

As we evolved, it turned out selling was our best research and development (R&D) process of all. The conversations we had with customers defined the way we built the product and informed every decision we made. That was the advantage of having a product so novel that we ourselves were learning how to describe it in conversations with customers. We'd try one way, and if that didn't land, we trotted out a new version, describing a category we were helping to create. The market made HourlyNerd more than we did. That would translate into instructions that we assiduously passed on to our IT team.

We had a few truly great strokes of luck. We had been introduced to the CEO of GE Ventures during the summer we were looking to raise angel funding, but at the time, she told us we were too early stage to interest GE. But out of the blue, only a few months later, Peter noticed that a senior leader from GE Global Innovation, a division of GE Ventures, had posted a project on our platform. We were all nervous that they were asking too much. They wanted to commercialize some of GE's robotics technologies and needed an expert who understood both the engineering and market of robotics. Within hours, the project had received several bids, including one from a Wharton MBA who had also written a dissertation on robotics while simultaneously earning an electrical engineering degree. What were the chances? At the time our paths crossed, he was teaching business at Boston College and was happy for the side gig. Three weeks later, the GE Ventures team had a deliverable in hand. The work had been completed much faster than they thought possible and had come in cheaper than they expected, costing a fraction of the fees charged by one of their usual consulting firms. They were pleased; we were ecstatic. From there we were off to the races with GE.

That was a gem of a deal, but more often than not it was a battle every step of the way. We'd get the phone call from the potential customer and sell them on the platform. Then Ben would help them scope the project and post it—and there the project would sit. Nerds would bid on it, but it was if the customer was afraid to pull the trigger. For a time we ran an iPad promotion, mailing a free iPad to any buyer that closed a project by month's end. We were starting to sound like Crazy Eddie, the madman electronics salesman made famous from New York in the 1970s. What's more, it was obviously not a good long-term strategy to give away a $400 iPad on a $5,000 deal that would only put $1,000 in our bank account. Still, we needed the business, and we hammered away using every trick up our sleeves. When we had a lead ready to convert, rather than wait for the customer to enter their credit card information into the site, we'd call them and offer to do it over the phone. As soon as anyone in our bullpen heard the words "credit card," the entire room went silent and all eyes became trained on the person talking on the phone. They'd tap in the numbers and hit enter. The moment the sale registered, we let out a cheer. They were the best of times and the worst of times. You had to wonder if Phil Knight went through the same thing every time he sold a pair of running shoes back in 1964. Running a start-up means always growing revenue month over month. There is no time to sleep, worry over blown deals, or assign blame when a good one went south. The sales treadmill was an ever-present force in our life, and it was a rare day in Boston that we ever hopped off.

When an important transaction did work out, like it did with GE Ventures, we banked on the assumption that momentum would grow and the market would do its thing. But we paid close attention to make sure. Especially in the early days, before we had attained critical mass and before we had the tech tools to help sort through experts, we made it our top priority to help businesses find the right expert. Sometimes that meant sifting through our own database by hand, or even reaching out to our personal networks to make the perfect match. We weren't going to let a big customer sit on the fence for long. If there was work to be done by an expert, it was our job to scan the web until we found the right person for the task. The expression "customer first" has not become obsolete in the tech age. We did whatever it took to ensure our customer was delighted with their HourlyNerd experience, end to end, and even when the machine was working effortlessly, we still were checking the nuts and bolts to minimize the possibility of a critical engagement going sour. It was a true example of spending time on "things that don't get scale" to avoid the ever-present specter of failure.

Deal maintenance became another task we assigned to our former intern and now head of client strategy. Ben let us know he had spoken to Bain and they had given him until the end of December to report to active duty in their Boston office. It was either that or he owed them nearly $200,000—to cover the $100,000-plus the firm had laid out in tuition, along with other payments, including bonuses. Ben was growing ever more indispensable to us, even as we knew we were going to lose him in a few months.

❈ ❈ ❈

It was a stifling, crazy-hot August day when another of our vital new recruits, Rich Gardner, showed up for his first day of work as our new head of sales. The elevator was on the fritz again, which meant sweating like you'd just run a marathon while trudging up the four flights of stairs to our offices. Rich had been a managing director at the Gerson Lehrmann Group, a New York–based company that matches hedge funds and other investment firms with industry experts. He had also served as the chief of fundraising for a large DC-based nonprofit. When he arrived at our office, he expected there be the usual slew of HR forms to fill out. Rich was in for plenty of surprises as he started with us. Rob showed him to a makeshift desk and said, "Here's where you sit. Now tell us what to do."

Rich had gone to Harvard undergrad and then Virginia Law. In his prior experience, he had sold to big professional services firms and closed on multimillion-dollar deals. He had agreed to leave the comfort of a large organization to join our growing operation, but early on he seemed to be having his doubts about us. Not long after joining, Rich seemed confused by Ben, who was both an intern, a chief strategist, and, to our thinking, probably the most valuable member of our sales team. At the end his first day, Rich met with us and said he thought our operation resembled the bar scene from the original *Star Wars*. We decided to take that as a compliment.

When Rich rolled up his sleeves and got down to business, he failed to see the logic in a strategy that had us selling to both the corner dry cleaner and General Electric in the same way. What we saw as eclectic and charming, he saw as convoluted—and that was probably a nice word for it. Rich explained to us that the value proposition for each was so different that focusing on both would only confuse his neophyte sales staff. We weren't as sure. From the outside, we seemed to be scoring some big wins in the second half of 2014. We did a project for a major big box retailer and gourmet food business—both recognizable brand names. We also worked with several lesser known brands with several hundred million dollars in sales. But we had to admit that we were all struggling with the right direction to channel our sales staff and its hodge-podge of expertise.

Rich was pushing us to aggressively move into enterprise sales. Rather than maintaining our current focus on small- and medium-sized businesses, he wanted us to train our sights on the Fortune 500. We understood his thinking. Successfully sell to a small business and they might post a project or two a year. But convince a larger business that there was value to our service and we could then sell 200 people—all with potential multiple projects—at one company. You didn't need a degree from MIT to follow that logic.

Somehow, we managed to keep Rich onboard, and he even began to recognize Ben's value; they struck up a serious friendship that continues unabated to this day. A few months after Rich started, he presented us with a plan that he and Ben had worked up. He wanted to employ at least a few people who would focus on nothing but big enterprise sales. He'd then assign them various sectors—health care, technology, industrials, retail—so they could gain deeper domain knowledge. He also proposed that we formalize what we had been doing informally, within the sales department. Junior people would be hired to prospect for leads in their designated industries. Each would be assigned to a more senior person, who would be brought on to do the actual selling and account hand-holding that we, as founders, had been doing. Eventually, we'd break each of the executive senior roles into two: some focused on sales while others served as account managers, whose job it would be to keep existing customers happy.

Not everyone agreed that we were ready to make the pivot to the enterprise. Other than Rich, none of us had the relationships that seemed necessary for selling into that particular category. There was also our stockpile of Nerds to consider. They were definitely of a caliber that could knock the socks off the owner of a regional manufacturing company or a small retail chain, but at the enterprise level they'd be competing with the armies of Bain and McKinsey.

There was also what in business school they call the "recency bias." We were seeing rapid growth in small business sales. We were seeing healthy growth among medium-sized businesses. By contrast, the enterprise had largely proven out of reach. Why not ride the small-to-medium-business (SMB) gravy train for a bit longer before devoting more resources to selling over our heads? We felt apprehensive about threatening the success that had gotten us this far. Sure, we had scored a win with GE Ventures, and that experience was proving worthwhile. But what if the power brokers inside the bigger firms had decided that we were a bargain they could ill afford? Devoting more resources to selling into big business meant paying less attention to the smaller businesses—and of course there was no guarantee that enterprise companies would ever move beyond a handful of smaller, quick-hit projects. Shifting our focus might actually cause a decline in sales, which could prove fatal for a small company like ours.

Though in retrospect the decision to zero in on the enterprise seems obvious, it was a serious dilemma for us in the summer of 2014. Rob embarked on a national speaking tour across Harvard Business School alumni clubs in the summer after graduation. Alumni were expecting in these sessions to hear the triumphant chest-beating of a successful HBS whiz kid, but instead they were asked to participate in an impromptu case discussion about which market segment made sense for HourlyNerd to pursue. Audiences in Pittsburgh, Phoenix, San Antonio, and Detroit, to name a few, vastly preferred the small business focus!

The state of our platform was another factor to consider. It wasn't quite enterprise ready, though at least our website was no longer an embarrassment. For that, we owe a debt of gratitude to our chief technology officer, Brian Morgan, who when he first met us, took one look at our dated website and asked, "Shouldn't you guys put some lipstick on that pig?" Pat, never one to back down from a challenge, took that as a dare and decided Brian was our guy. Brian had other intentions and for all practical purposes, said no to our first offer. What followed was six months of constant emailing, to which we were rejected again and again. At least he was nice about it. He said we were a bunch of B-school guys who didn't know the first thing about technology—but he thought our idea wasn't awful and he did wish us luck.

By April, undaunted, Pat had broken him down and thought he had the deal in hand when he and Peter took Brian to a home-town Celtics basketball game. Excellent Celtics tickets are hard to come by. Despite Pat and Peter's impassioned pitch, Brian still demurred. Now Rob was as energized as Pat. Good seats had been wasted. This deal had to close.

On a Tuesday, we knew Brian was taking his wife and three daughters to Disney World. So we made him an offer. Which he refused again. Pat decided to ramp it up. "Dude, I think you're making a mistake," Pat told him. "This is the right fit; you should be joining us. We're going to be huge. There is no reason for you not to come along for the ride unless you're scared. You want to go work at a big company, go work at a big company. A person who lets fear dictate his decisions should be at a big, big company. You're making a mistake. Go on your vacation, think about it. If the job is still here when you get back, maybe we can talk then." Pat reported his pitch back to us. We made a mental note not to put him in charge of employee relations.

That week we knew Brian was somewhere on the grounds of the Disney Resort. The only problem was they have close to a dozen hotel properties. So we took it upon ourselves to call them all until we had what we hoped was a confirmation on his room number. We found a Disney service company that would go into your hotel room and decorate the hell out of it. We really couldn't afford nonsense like this, but at this point we had no choice. We went whole hog: stuffed animals, streamers, buckets of candy for the kids, champagne for the grown-ups. We waited all day for The Call. Nothing. Had we pushed too hard? Did the guy think we were stalking him? Deliverance came in the form of a midnight text. Attached was a photo of his smiling kids in full Mickey Mouse regalia buried under a mountain of candy. The next morning we had our CTO.

The team was building but we still had core positions to fill. Not trivial but a little less stressful was filling the CIO role. Retaining Bryan Stevenson as CIO was probably easier, in spite of his alternative opportunities, because he came onboard later, when we had some nice successes (and quite a few more fundraises) to show off. Pat first met Bryan when he spoke at one of our HBS classes. He thought the guy was a rare example of an actual, dyed-in-the-wool genius. He told him what we were doing, but Bryan had already started his own company called InsightSquared. We were stymied yet again. "After I sell my company I'm never going to join another start-up," he told us. We reached out a year later and he would not relent. But we finally got him to listen in on one of our sales calls, and a light went on. Bryan had trained for 18 months as a sales guy just to hone his leadership skills for whatever later life dished up. His response to the call was: "Holy hell, I've never heard a customer want anything that badly. I've never seen an easier sale." We had our Brian-driven technology team in place.

After new CTO Brian finally signed on the dotted line, the first thing he did was redo the website and update the marketing pages. Meanwhile, his small team rebuilt the site and our whole look from the ground up. The most amazing part is that there wasn't a moment we were offline as Brian seamlessly switched the company over. It was as if he were performing open-heart surgery on a beating, living website. A lot of what we were doing back then was like fixing the plane while it was flying.

At that point, we gave Rich the green light to implement his sales plan. If our technology could catch up, so then would the team we had assembled. We also considered our database of Nerds and decided we had confidence in our ability to attract the experts we would need to satisfy the demands of bigger customers. Members of our board had considerable enterprise experience, and they had been encouraging us to take the risk. The economics of selling to the enterprise also proved persuasive. The cost of attracting an SMB to the site was relatively small, but so was the lifetime value of that customer. Securing a large business as a customer might ultimately be costly, but they would also be potentially lucrative—to the tune of tens or even hundreds of millions. This was a risk we deemed eminently takeable. Once we got the ball rolling, the network effect and the virality could only be a good thing. One big buyer parlays into two or three referrals. We play that into a case study. Folks start talking about it at the water cooler. "Hey, where did you get this partner research report? It's really good." "That was HourlyNerd. You guys should check them out. Here's the link!"

Bingo! We started getting testimonials, and this beautiful cycle began where the more social groups we amassed, the less pain was required to seal the deal with new customers. Customer 10 costs us less to acquire than customer 2, because they see that we're working together with eight of their colleagues. The risk goes away very materially for potential new clients just by not being the first one to do it. This is the case for a lot of disruptive businesses. You draw early adopters, and these people seem to have social capital. Doing a first project at a big company and then waving that flag at any champion we could find leads to more engagements: "Have you done work with HourlyNerd before? It went great? Fantastic. Let's talk!"

Our enthusiasm for beefing up our enterprise presence did not mean we would turn our back on small businesses, however. They were our bread and butter and kept our experts busy, which was critical to the health of the HourlyNerd ecosystem. We simply were expanding our horizons, setting our sights on a much richer target: the globe's largest corporations. Which did not mean that it was going to be easy.

We also saw some surprising results from our early, junior sales team. Massachusetts natives Pat Kneeland and John Nylen were our first and second sales employees. Both joined us a few years out of college, with very little relevant experience. Nevertheless, they showed an incredible hunger and appetite for learning and continuous improvement. After an incredibly successful time opening doors at key enterprises, Pat left us for business school at Georgetown in the fall of 2015. John remained and grew up through the ranks, eventually formally launching and successfully growing a mid-market enterprise business that accounted for much of our key growth in the early years. John remembered of the early years, "I learned to expect the unexpected and know better than to underestimate what the company can accomplish in short periods of time. The common thread weaving through my early memories was how violently we celebrated as a team regardless of the magnitude of the milestone—whether it was posting a $192 project for a start-up or closing a six-figure engagement for a Fortune 10. The victories were sweet because of the blood, sweat, and tears we poured into each day. The team's passion and dedication to the mission has always been the constant."

Retail office supply giant Staples was one of those celebrated early enterprise wins. They came on board during our SMB days when we were still refining our business model. We got our foot in the door through pure hustle and persistence, with a sprinkle of good business judgment. Our first Staples projects were low-dollar, quick-turnaround revisions to marketing collateral and client presentations, not exactly C-suite strategy recommendations. "Help us make this deck a little better. Polish up this presentation." Not mission critical stuff. But that was the price of admission, and successful outcomes on these projects earned us a seat at the table with ever more senior stakeholders, which in turn led to introductions to bigger project buyers, which enabled bigger project sales. We felt the snowball effect: that one moment when a bunch of good conversations crystalize into serious sales momentum.

* * *

The myth of today's CEO culture casts that person as a chief wizard forever spinning out brilliant ideas—a Midas of start-up innovation with a seemingly endless toolkit of skills that perhaps none of us have. We don't doubt there are companies where the CEO wears the hat of head of product development and chief software engineer and regularly shoots a 68 in Pebble Beach. But our experience was leading us to think that Jack Dorsey, who those days served as chief executive of both Twitter and Square, was onto something when he said the job of the CEO is to create a vision, hire great people, and never run out of money. We were all over that. And we added one more item to that list: the CEO also needs to be responsible for the workplace culture.

Company culture has always been a preoccupation of ours. Maybe that's because none of us had ever been a boss before and here we were now, grad students running our own shop. It's like we had no choice but to pay special attention once we started hiring people. We knew the things we *didn't* like about being someone's employee. The crazy hours. The middle managers who make you feel like an input to their promotion path. Out-of-balance lives that were all about work and little else. Among the lot of us, we'd had enough bad experiences (among various good) to know what we didn't want—not for ourselves and not for our employees. And it wasn't just the group we had already assembled that we were worried about. What people say about you on the street spreads like wildfire in this culture. People think your bright new start-up is the place to be and recruitment is a manager's dream. If the word gets out that you squeeze the rind too hard and send folks out wishing they had never met you, that's not good. We didn't want to become exactly the kind of workplace our Nerds were trying to avoid. So we basically designed the company to be the kind of place where we'd want to work. There was no engraved set of principles, no cheesy woodcut of our values superimposed against a yawing sailboat on the Charles. But we knew who we were, and that credo was unmistakably stamped into our culture.

That did not mean 80-hour workweeks in a loft chockfull of pool tables and refrigerators full of energy drinks, craft beer, and designer water. We were still new, still hungry, and we expected and wanted our people to be as hungry and enthused as we were, but without killing them or burning them out. The established culture had us welcoming a lot of newcomers who were accustomed to the 80-hour workweek, and even thought that was for slackers since anyone worth their salt from Wall Street or Big Consulting clocked a hundred. We had worked in jobs like that, too, and understood from experience that nobody was at their best when they put in those kind of hours. It was on us to establish our own unique culture and find a middle ground between forced labor versus sloughing off.

We also recognized that if we were serious about pushing a new paradigm, it would take time to fully realize anything close to our vision. So like everything else, we had to learn on the fly. We encouraged people to work five days a week, not seven, and we actually meant it. Ten to 12-hour days felt like a fair norm. The three of us often worked a lot more hours than that, as did the other executives on our management team. We modeled a strong enthusiasm for the job, but we didn't ram it down anyone's throats. That kind of muscle was for someone else's start-up. Our goal was a workforce that wouldn't feel hosed if they found themselves in the office for a considerable amount of time. We weren't punching time cards, but we hoped that the newcomers would give a super-focused and intense 50 hours of hard work and feel rewarded in the process. Fifty hours when you are inspired doesn't feel like that much. If it's drudgery, it's a lifetime. So far, we seemed to have struck a fair balance.

People worked hard, but we also made sure that they enjoyed coming to the Nerd factory every day. We made a conscious effort to balance the seriousness of the mission with some good old-fashioned fun. One day, to celebrate a massive revenue milestone, we brought everyone into the conference room under the guise of a key strategy meeting. Then we announced the great number had been achieved, handed out goggles, garbage bags, and bottles of champagne, and celebrated like the Red Sox had just won the World Series. The payoff was palpable. We hosted the occasional blowout at a local karaoke bar and often held epic rock-paper-scissor tournaments on moments like our second anniversary as a company. Rob, of all people, often led the fun, and we found ourselves cut loose in the middle of a great and competitive group of people. They were exactly the kind of staff we'd imagined when we decided this was going to be the antidote to the bleak corporate existence we were so desperate to avoid.

Lots of start-ups claimed to have a low-key, laid-back culture, and at times you could sense there was a forced nature to whole affair—the sort of environment that was ripe for a *Saturday Night Live* skit. We prided ourselves on being as silly and juvenile as the next guy, and we had no shame about playing pranks in between the daily angst. One early employee was positively territorial about keeping a cache of his own snacks at his space. Unfortunately, we had an epidemic of mice in the office, which was a less than favorable environment for stowing one's edible goodies. The guy had an epic stash of candy and cakes that every last one of us knew he kept hidden away in Tupperware containers stowed in the bottom of a beat-up old file cabinet. Pat, who saw no affront as too off-the-wall, actually went out and scored a look-alike Tupperware container, drilled a hole in one corner, and worked it over with a screwdriver until it looked exactly like a mouse had eaten through it. For good measure, he took small bits of a Tootsie Roll, rolled them between his fingers so they resembled mouse turds, and switched his booby trap out with the employee's container. The poor guy was so freaked out that he screwed up the courage to bring his container into our office and complain about our suspect sanitation habits. Pat took a look at the container, examined the "mouse turds," and then popped one in his mouth! "Yup, mouse turd," he told the guy. We were probably one step from losing a talented worker, but sometimes you just had to not take this stuff too seriously. Being tasked with changing the face of the workplace and starting a company is a heavy load. Taking a little time out for play said a lot about who we were. At least, so we hoped.

❀ ❀ ❀

Our small company was growing. We started using more sophisticated sales-based forecasting tools and added performance management dashboards. With Rich's help, we reworked our pitch decks and remade other sales collateral.

That was the easy stuff compared to the challenge Rich had given himself. His first priority, of course, was making his monthly number. He would press his team to bang the phones hour after hour, every single day, and convince people at the companies we had signed on to post on the site. It wasn't enough to have a powerful starting lineup. We had to deliver the hits, and Rich took that personally and seriously. He compounded his challenge by letting go of a couple of junior employees he'd inherited from us because he didn't see them as up to the job. Meanwhile, he spent much of each day searching for new, inspired salespeople who would let him execute on his idea that the enterprise was our future. We never quite knew what he considered the secret sauce to enterprise success, but you had to hand it to the guy—he was thoughtful and deliberate about how he brought people on.

The junior people were easier to find. Just look for recent college graduates who had the hunger to cold-call prospects who had no idea what they were selling. The only sticking point here was the training piece. We weren't selling Ginsu knives. Rich had to designate rapid-fire, on-the-job sales training protocols for a product no one had any experience with. But he filled desks, the calls got made, and we rang up the numbers.

The real challenge was in finding the right senior salespeople for this particular product. Rich decided to focus on former consultants—people like Ben, who had spent years working with enterprise customers. There was a special knack to instinctually understanding the problems confronting the people inside the enterprise. You had to custom-tell the story that would illustrate the ways that the HourlyNerd platform could help these big entities, especially when they were accustomed to the (overpriced) hand-holding of a firm like BCG or McKinsey. Rich needed people who understood that they were selling solutions, not a product.

Reaching into the enterprise presented any number of challenges, starting with the person you needed to get on the phone. Usually that was pretty obvious at a smaller company. But the larger companies were wallpapered with layers of vice presidents and regional chieftains. Where did you start? Who did you target? How did you even find the right person who might know the right person, and then convince them to take your call based on a 15-second pitch?

Through trial and error, we discovered that our best bets for any sort of stickiness inside the corporation were the people at the director level—the director of finance, say, or marketing or strategy. They were busy people with a lot on their plates, but also the ones to most directly feel the frustration of putting out fires with a binary choice: do things in-house when they needed extra firepower on a project or engage a large consulting firm that meant paying fees in the hundreds of thousands, if not millions. We decided our value proposition was empowerment. We were offering a third option—a way to solve a problem without blowing a huge hole in their budget.

There was, however, an irony in selling empowerment to employees inside a large corporation. Often the very people most desperate for a platform like ours didn't have the power to start using it. When selling to small businesses, the person on the phone was usually the one who said "yes" and wrote the check. Not so in the enterprise. Our salespeople rarely had a chance to speak with the person who could ultimately sign off on a deal. No matter how much an SVP liked our platform and our value proposition, the purchasing director might prove dubious about engaging with a tiny company. Legal might be the kibosh on the whole thing because of the terms of an NDA, or an executive vice president might just say no because saying no was part of his job description. Companies that boast about innovation aren't always so quick to innovate. Blowing a million bucks on a big consulting contract was the way of the business world. Those yesses were handed out like candy. But blowing $50,000 on a deal with a start-up website run by a handful of people no one had ever heard of? One misstep there and that could kill a career.

That would prove to be one of the more surprising lessons from our on-the-job training: even the most powerful executives inside many U.S. corporations can feel utterly powerless.

Several early wins, however, helped convince us we were on the right path, none more so than a $50,000 project with a global oil giant. The company had recently shifted its strategy strongly, resulting in distribution challenges for a small but important part of its historical business. Management was prepared to engage a large firm to find a solution, but we had other plans.

We emailed, we called, we hustled any way we could to get on the calendar of our contact within the company. We threw everything we had at scoping the project, and identifying the right experts, and pricing it competitively to ensure success. We flew down to see the client three times, working over weekends and Labor Day. We were so green at this game that Rob, one of the cofounders of our company, personally helped Ben hammer out a 10-page scoping presentation to rival any of the Big 3. Finally, after we'd exhausted every creative ounce of firepower, we got a seven-word response from the client. "Let's do this! When do we start?" It was our biggest deal to date and our first Fortune 100 customer after GE.

✢ ✢ ✢

The great irony of landing the massive oil company deal was that it was Ben, our interning head of client strategy, who was the most instrumental in bringing in the deal. We beat ourselves senseless patting one another on the back for our acumen, bringing such a talented young guy into the fold, even as we prepared to lose him. Nobody leaves $200,000 of student loans (and almost guaranteed future success) on the table to work at a low-paying start-up.

We were wondering about his departure date when he rounded us up to make an announcement. He had given his decision a lot of thought over the preceding months and had decided he'd stay with us. We double-checked to confirm he was sure before we applauded him for his choice and mentally canceled a going-away party. Prior to working at HourlyNerd, Ben would have described himself as fairly risk-averse. But Bain was predictable and we were not—and wasn't that what the whole HourlyNerd mandate was all about? Ben decided to shake it up and we were glad for it, though we sure as heck didn't want to be on the call to his parents announcing he was giving up Bain to work for a company with the word "Nerd" in the title. And to be fair, it had to be an even more difficult call to the Bain partners who had treated him so well. Sure, they'd get their hefty loan back. But they had also invested in someone they believed in. Ben's respect for the firm and for what it had provided him made the decision that much more tortuous. When he'd originally committed to Bain, it was in good faith. It wasn't the Bain people that Ben was rejecting. It was the career consultant's way of life. In this stage of his career, he was no longer authentically able to commit himself to Bain with the level of buy-in that he figured his employer deserved. In many ways his choice exemplified everything we were about. One could choose to "do work differently," and Ben was taking that risk.

He would explain this all to us over a celebration and business planning dinner. Ben didn't mess around, and we liked that about him, too. In retrospect, it was a crafty strategy for a guy who inherited a daunting student loan but would eventually become our VP of Strategy. If he was worried about throwing himself into bankruptcy before he turned 30, it never showed. Instead, he clapped his hands together, rolled up his sleeves, and set out on the path to help fundamentally define the future of work.

CHAPTER 9

The Upside-Down Work/Life Equation

Winter–Spring–Summer 2015

I would've used this 10 times over in each of my last two companies if I'd known if this had existed. This is brilliant.

—AMY VILLENEUVE, FORMER PRESIDENT AND COO OF KIVA SYSTEMS, A DIVISION OF AMAZON, ADVISOR, CATALANT TECHNOLOGIES

It was sunny. Pat remembers that about the day. It was mid-afternoon, and he was at a café near the office, having an iced coffee with a junior member of the sales force who had requested the meeting. The day was so nice that the two decided to sit at an outside table. The year was 2015, and we were growing at a ferocious pace. The idea of the casual coffee with the boss was something that we encouraged. We tended to attract the aggressive types to our ranks, and we'd grown accustomed to this reverse interview dialectic. This would be her opportunity to pump one of us for information.

"Five years from now," she asked Pat, "where do you see the company?"

The truth of the matter is none of us would have known how to answer that question. Anything we might have said back then would have been suspect. But leave it to Pat to respond by winging an answer that we're still talking about years later. Our young salesperson had asked about the company's future, but he responded as if she had asked the proverbial "where-do-you-see-yourself-in-five-years" interview question.

"I think this whole idea of career dictating your life is messed up," he began in classic Pat style. "It should be flipped on its head. Life first, and then career fits in." He asked her to imagine what she'd been dreaming about when she was a youngster. She stared at him.

"Everything they told you in school, that thing that all the adults ask," she replied. "What do you want to be when you grow up?"

Pat bore down. "It's like you're brainwashed from the time you're a little kid to think about this and then they tell you that you have to go find a career?" He was on a roll.

"You go to college and you graduate and then you get a job with a company that says, 'Go live in this city.' So now the job dictates who you're friends with, how close or far away you are from your family, who you end up meeting and marrying—and so your whole life is determined by what city this company happened to tell you to go live in?"

Maybe it was the long hours he had been working that week. Or perhaps it was the contrast between the good feeling of the sun on his face in the middle of a beautiful Boston afternoon and the darkness of the tale he was unspooling. Pat brought up the stories we'd all heard of: people putting off having kids for a job, the relationships destroyed because corporate moved you to Kansas City when the love of your life was in Fort Lauderdale. "It's like every decision you make in your life is dictated by the company. It's this impersonal corporation that creates the framework and barriers you're forced to live with in your life until the day you retire. What about the guy who works at a company for 50 years and drops dead three weeks after his farewell party? How depressing is that?" We'd all grown quiet. Pat really knew how to light up a room.

"There's got to be a better idea for work than that."

Every company has its legends. And there are moments that get passed down from generation to generation. It's been going on since the days of Henry Ford. It is the stuff of the American workplace. Inside a different company than ours, Pat's soliloquy might have simply been a fun rant that employees shared, likely when Pat was out of town or at least out of the office—at a Red Sox game or doing yoga or whatever Pat did those days to keep his blood pressure down. The boss takes a newish employee out for coffee and welcomes her with a curse-laden tirade about work not being nearly as important as people think. Next!

But for us, it became a kind of company mantra, or at least the preamble to the closest thing we had to one. Our first step had been to create the platform that liberates the worker. Work hard, sure, but you don't have to sacrifice life and liberty to do so. The next step—the game-changer—would come about once businesses recognized that the same human cloud technologies that were powering the broader gig economy had the potential to transform the workplace. That's where we figured we were jumping into the game.

* * *

Looking back on our humble beginnings, we never set out to change the way people inside large corporations got things done. There were systems in place. We got jobs within those frameworks and we played along for a while, and then we didn't. We thought there might be a better way. We had no great vision about the future of work. We merely stumbled on it while trying to grow our small company. In those early days, we had one goal: convince businesses to post tasks on our website. The rest—the product, the sales pitch, the vision—grew from a rabid belief in listening to customers and learning from what they had to say. It was the customers who pointed the way to a very different view of work that goes way beyond casual Fridays and free snacks. Pretty much everyone inside our growing company spoke to customers. Any one of us could have told you things weren't quite right inside corporate America. But it was Pat who had the idea of taking this window of opportunity we had and digging deeper. Why not ask customers more directly why they use us? We had nothing to lose. Pat was fearless. A little truth, good or bad, could only help our cause. So began our period of customer-driven, intensive self-evaluation.

It started with customers telling us the obvious: that they used Catalant when they didn't have the right person in-house to get something done. In the past, they had turned to an expensive consultancy—the usual suspects—but now they were using us.

Our first big surprise came next, when we asked if they thought we were disrupting the consulting business. We expected them to say yes, but that did not prove to be the case. We weren't so much an alternative to established consulting firms, they said, but instead a bright light shining on a deeper problem. "You're disrupting the root cause of why we purchase consulting in the first place," one customer said. His company viewed consulting as a way of bringing in outsiders to help them think through a problem. He wondered, what if they could skip over the problem and eliminate the need for consulting in the first place?

Our clients were starting to view us as a way to bring a diversity of talent into their company that they couldn't otherwise recruit into their ranks. This particular company was not located in one of the big urban centers known for its cache of knowledge workers, say like a New York or a Boston or San Francisco. They were in a less-served destination that, frankly, was having trouble attracting and retaining top head count. And here we were providing them with a way of gaining access to those very same people who had proven unwilling to relocate to their corporate headquarters. "We think of you," one customer memorably said, "as a way of bringing great people into our company that we couldn't otherwise have."

We had started Catalant thinking we were democratizing consulting services for small businesses. Moving up the stack, we saw ourselves as disrupting consulting inside the enterprise. But larger businesses saw us differently: as a way of tapping into a wider pool of talent. We were providing them with a way to harness the brainpower of those who might not be willing to uproot themselves and move to Indianapolis or Dallas, no matter how lovely or desirable those cities might be. We were giving businesses a way of expanding their workforce without adding to their employee head count or overhead.

We got it. The message was coming through loud and clear. Whenever we dove into our growing pool of experts, we were amazed by the caliber of the resumes people were posting on our site. Our human capital coffers were populated by the sorts of workers we had never thought of as part of the freelance economy. These were men and women who had spent 5 or 10 years at McKinsey. They had earned a PhD or MBA from a top-tier university yet were choosing to work independently because they could. Maybe they had worked for a few years at a Google or a PayPal or a Facebook, but now they were on the hunt for interesting projects.

Honestly, we've been in awe of our experts since day 1. We seemed to have drawn some of the most interesting, highest-quality people around. If you dug into their resumes, you discovered that they had been invited to guest lecture at leading business schools and speak at exclusive conferences. Their papers had been published and their professional exploits honored by all sorts of respected organizations. Because of their extensive references, they were able to charge top dollar to the customers who engaged them on our site, but that was still just a fraction of what established consulting firms would have charged for their services, given their overhead and other costs. We were impressed, so it was no surprise that our customers were impressed, too. These were smart companies with an appetite for value, and they could do the math. If you could gain access to the best people in a wide range of professional fields at a fraction of what it would cost to hire someone full-time or enlist a consultant firm, why not?

"Artisanal" is normally a term applied to cheese. Really good, expensive cheese coaxed from very special, pampered goats leading a life of blissful peace on a hillside in Vermont. The word had spread south, to the hipster communal urban farmer living in Williamsburg, Brooklyn, who had revived the lost art of distilling hops or brining the perfect pickle. (In fact, plenty of those artisan food makers in Brooklyn had also abandoned the consulting life for a better existence.) But we were discovering there was also a kind of artisanal freelancer making themselves known to the marketplace. These were people with a special skill set (and mind-set!) that allows them to charge a premium for their services. They sat on top of the job food chain and, because they could generally run circles around most everyone else, had the temerity to live as Pat imagined people should. They used their hard-earned skills to hang a shingle and enlist with the gig economy, thus buying their freedom and taking control of their life. Maybe they were just born with this supreme confidence and had come of age in an era that did not value long-term employment. Or perhaps they had been tested by the old economy and circumstance had forced their hand. Either way, they had turned to freelancing because they were talented and confident enough to know they could make it on their own. And they were flocking to Catalant and finding work and satisfaction, which, no surprise, garnered high praise and top ratings from the businesses that had found them through our platform. Maybe there was something to this work/life balance after all, because all of a sudden, both customer and worker were a pretty happy lot.

We were a restless management team, however, and we took nothing for granted. We kept probing whenever we had the chance. Listening to customers and understanding their pain points was almost a religion with us. Over time, we heard one familiar lament over and over again. Company workloads vary, but the full-time employee census stays the same. Adding capacity was almost impossible in today's cost-cutting environment, and even if it were possible to bump your head count when work demanded, once it slipped off again, paring down during slower times would be painful and demoralizing to the remaining staff.

There was another factor that played to our cause. Polls showed that barely one-third of the country's corporate executives thought graduates were workforce ready.[1] In other words, we were building an asset that management didn't even know exists. They knew they had a problem, that much was for sure. Workflow fluctuates with the time of year. People go on maternity leave. Others get sick and need a few months to recover. Management wanted access to flexible talent when they needed it, we were told by one stressed-out executive after another. But instead they were stuck with the troops they had, all of them locked in a rigid, unchallenged system that trapped workers and hurt the bottom line.

Eventually, we figured out that through our database of skilled Nerds, we were in effect digitizing talent on behalf of the globe's businesses. Corporations were desperate for the right mix of people, but they had few options to turn to for a quick solution. Consultants provided an expensive roster of generalists, but the consulting solution was slow, costly, and unwieldy. Consulting firms had big infrastructure to support. They had to charge what they did. Our experts could be making cheese on a hillside one afternoon and then working on a high-end gig for the next three weeks for a company with a problem that needed solving. That company didn't need to support an expensive network of global offices to land one skilled set of hands with a brain. They didn't

---

[1] Joe Fuller.

need to go through a lengthy interview process. As remarkable as it seemed to our customers at first, we had what they needed, it worked, and it did so at a fraction of the cost.

❆ ❆ ❆

Transforming ourselves into a true B-to-B enterprise that sold into global companies was expensive. It cost money to poach top talent from the globe's top consulting firms to build our burgeoning sales team. There was also the cost of morphing from an open matchmaking website to a platform robust and secure enough for large-sized companies. The tech team was also expanding, so we had to factor in the price of retooling the platform to make it enterprise-worthy.

There was no doubt we were taking the business in a more serious direction, and that meant it was time for us to raise a Series B round of venture money.

The good news is that we were in the midst of a giant growth spurt at just the right time. The back half of 2014 had proven a boon for the business. The bad news was the macroeconomic tremors that were spooking the broader market. The stock market dropped nearly 500 points in a single morning in October of 2014.[2] We were talking about selling to the country's largest companies, and the Standard and Poor's 500 stock index saw a 7 percent drop in value that fall.[3]

In retrospect, we should have done a much bigger Series A and given ourselves more time. Instead, we were faced with the need to fundraise at a critical strategic moment. This period would need to be about execution. Rich needed to build his staff, but it was even more pressing that he hit his numbers, knowing that VCs would be looking at our books. Once again, we'd need to

---

[2]Matt Egan, October 2015, Market "freak out": Stocks rebound from scary plunge, http://money.cnn.com/2014/10/15/investing/stocks-markets-wall-street-correction/.

[3]From a September high of 2,004 to a low in mid-October of 1,865.

put thoughtful planning and big-picture strategic thinking on hold as we devoted our time to fundraising.

There were fun aspects to the B round, no doubt generated by the success we'd been having in our first couple of years. Pat and Rob flew out to the West Coast one weekend on a few hours' notice to have breakfast on a Sunday morning in Silicon Valley with Intuit cofounder Scott Cook. He had used our platform, he told us, and had only good experiences. The breakfast—which was amazing, by the way—ended with Scott telling us, "Whenever you guys are ready, I'm good for $500,000 or a million. Just let me know." We'd be remiss not to warn beginners: don't try this at home. Not everyone rings up results like this so easily and so early on. Our roll continued with equally great get-togethers with former Etsy CEO Maria Thomas and Rent the Runway founder Jennifer Hyman, both of whom also wanted to invest in the company. Then, upon our return to home base in Boston, we had the thrill of meeting members of the Kraft family, who owned the New England Patriots. Jonathan Kraft had already let us know that his family was interested in investing next time we raised money. We were now able to invite them into the company.

We announced our Series B financing in February of 2015. Highland Capital again led the round—a great vote of confidence from the first venture firm willing to take a chance with us. Greylock's Bill Helman was also pleased with the progress we were making because his firm, too, put up more money in the B round. All told, we raised $7.8 million. Rounding out our list of investors were GE Ventures, a customer and now partner in building the company, and Semil Shah, who had founded Haystack, a Silicon Valley–based early-stage investment firm. We may have planted some roots now in the Silicon Valley, but there was no denying the thrill of opening the *Boston Globe* to find a story about our funding round in the local business pages. The article included a picture of the three of us, but the real excitement was captured by a quote from the Kraft family: "Though pretty active in funding start-ups, rarely, if ever, publicly, do the Krafts lend its name to its investments. Which says a lot about how highly Jonathan and Daniel Kraft think of HourlyNerd." In our small-town minds, we had just taken the field with Tom Brady. Some dreams actually do come true.

* * *

While our aspirations were sky-high, and even a lot of our management execution was spot-on, we still were a tiny start-up selling business services to other businesses—your classic B-to-B. There were areas where we needed help, and mining the existing workplace for some crystalline innovation in marketing was no easy feat. Sure, there were plenty of great people out there, but they were full-time employed and launching and reinventing products for soft drinks and smartphones, killer apps and social networks. It was a challenge for us to dredge the waters for some talent to ignite our feisty little start-up in the marketing arena. But we had the humility to recognize that we couldn't do everything ourselves.

Our first marketing maven, Devon Petersmeyer Johnson, came to us from a major personal grooming brand where she had been dealing with national campaigns, and frankly, we weren't sure we would close the deal. We still remember what she said during our initial meeting in our conference room in the midst of a classic New England blizzard. "The room was just vibrating with excitement," she recalled. "A group of smart people struggling with tough questions, working together and getting their hands dirty to build something great. For me that was super-energizing."

Peter—a banker by training and our CFO—*had* been our de facto head of marketing through the first two years of the company. We had hired a junior person to take some of the weight off his shoulders and manage social media and a future-of-work blog we had launched. And of course we had the platform for when we needed help developing marketing materials. But finally hiring a tried and tested head of marketing proved to be a great move. We were starting to feel like a grown-up company, even if at that point each of us was struggling to make sure we had clean socks for work each day.

* * *

Reaching into the enterprise had its challenges. The sale that might take a few weeks now took several months, if not longer. The main complaint from our potential enterprise customers was that we were running an open market and not a proprietary network that they, or we, could control. Some weren't comfortable being on the same marketplace as competitors. Others were concerned about doing business on the same platform that neighbored with a local shop down the street. Brian's tech team worked on solutions while our budding enterprise sales force worked hard at convincing big companies to give us a chance. The change in focus seemed to be working. In February of 2014, the goal had been $80,000 in revenue. By June of 2015, we had booked more than $1 million. The numbers were speaking louder than our biggest fears. We might have been doing something right.

That summer, Rich implemented a "pod" structure for his group that had us organizing the sales team by industry. Pat Mascia, who we had poached from the consulting firm Vantage Partners, took over industrials (manufacturing, chemicals), as well as health care. A former McKinsey person would be hired to focus on technology companies. Pat Griffin, a former Bain consultant, took over retail. "A lot of that first year was about crafting our story, so it made sense to enterprise customers," he said. In a way, his own journey was instructive. When he first heard of us while at Bain, he thought, "That's cute." At Bain, they assigned a team of four or six people to a problem and charged as much as $1 million a month. In time, Pat came to see us as "the Johnny Appleseed of a different kind of consulting."

In September 2015, we moved to Fort Point, the epicenter of the tech scene in Boston.[4] Consistent with our do-it-yourself attitude, and our preference to only spend money on growth, Pat and Peter cleaned out our old office themselves and moved everything to the new office (with the help of several other employees).[5] Our new neighborhood, officially dubbed the Seaport Innovation District, was also where our friends from GE would very soon relocate. Others were following fast afoot. For us, our Summer Street offices meant that for the first time we were in a building with an automated elevator—each of our previous offices had had a manual freight elevator. As luck would have it, the office also came fully furnished. The previous tenant had needed to vacate the space quickly so threw in its desks, chairs, and quite a few accoutrements we would have been far too cheap to buy. It was a nice problem to have, and while we didn't get to pick our own carpeting, we were more than happy to benefit from their largesse. Because the office was pre-furnished, we were able to spring it on employees as a big surprise one warm September Boston afternoon.

As we added more salespeople, we had more wins to share, and that in turn inspired future customers with our growing and impressive roster. An executive with a Fortune 100 company contacted us on a Friday. They needed a white paper by the end of the following week. By Monday morning, they had connected through the site to a Harvard MBA in Chicago with precisely the right domain expertise to pull off the assignment in five days. These kind of breakneck deadlines looked really good for us if we could nail them. The Nerd who took on the task delivered on time, the client was thrilled, and so were we. No matter that it had been only a

---

[4]Rebecca Strong, February 2015, Map: Tech Companies of Fort Point http://bostinno.streetwise.co/2015/02/12/innovation-district-boston-fort-point-tech-companies-map/.

[5]Rob was lucky to be at his sister's college graduation.

$2,000 assignment. It was a baby toe in the water for us with a company with $50 billion a year in revenues. It would prove the first of many projects they posted to our site.

Another multinational in the Fortune 100 received a $2 million bid from one of the big management consulting firms for a data visualization project. Through our site, they found a former McKinsey project manager with a PhD in mechanical engineering now running his own firm specializing in data visualization. Go figure! It was a classic example of our ability to disrupt an age-old model and provide true value. Ringing up these kinds of wins electrified our sales team and provided a continued boost to our revenue stream.

We were also edging our way into the Fortune 1000 by offering new ways for customers to tackle old problems. In late 2015, a fabled computer manufacturer came to us. In the old days, which is to say the year before they met us, they would have turned to one of the big consulting firms, which probably would have thrown a team of six at the problem and started the meter at $250,000 a month. Instead, the customer opted to divvy the project up into four smaller ones and leverage our platform to find a different consultant for each task. Good news for everyone: they ended up with the right person with precisely the right skill set without paying the whopping overhead of a big firm—and we booked new business.

One of our most dramatic early wins, and certainly one of the largest outside of GE Ventures, came from a global agricultural and industrial giant. They needed to better understand grain production in Eastern Europe and turned to one of the Big 3 for a proposal. However, the consulting firm rejected the assignment, citing local security concerns. Through our site, we connected the customer with several Stanford MBA graduates who had set up a small firm in Romania and were more than happy to take on the task. The MBAs rolled up their sleeves and got to work, delivering the goods in a timely fashion. They delighted the customer and happily earned $40,000 for a month of work on their report. The customer was just happy that someone was able to deliver. And in addition to bolstering our reputation and adding a valuable new client, we gained a shot of confidence. Not only did we now know experts in Eastern European grain production, but we were getting traction in the manner that most mattered. We weren't just booking business. Like Amazon in the early days indexing the world of retailers, we were indexing the world of smart people available for project-based work.

* * *

At an off-site during the blur of 2015, we debated the utility of Pat's rant about the upside-down nature of the work/life equation. Rob—the nerdiest of us—understood the potential broad appeal but didn't appreciate the desire for flexibility as much. He liked weekend golf and Patriots games in the fall, but he liked work an awful lot, too. He had been willing to move when Bain Capital offered him a job, and he remained in Boston when it was the deemed the only place HourlyNerd could be built. Peter was skeptical that the market was ready to accept this massive paradigm shift. But we all recognized the power of what Pat was saying.

Some people needed the security of a permanent job. We weren't about to decimate the U.S. workplace, not by any stretch. Others probably didn't have the resume to compete on a platform like ours. And then there were those who might favor the work/life balance we imagined, but they had a personality for a different kind of solution. We all need good cheese.

We knew we weren't for everyone. But as our systems and database ramped up, it became clear we were sitting on a technology that could offer freedom to millions, if not tens of millions of workers worldwide. And just in case we ever doubted it, we had Joe Fuller, the Harvard management professor who serves as a Catalant board observer, to reiterate the truth. We were generating the types of employment opportunities that were so hard for independent professionals to access on their own.

Pat, of course, had his own analysis of the situation: "Imagine an alien came down and visited Earth and could immediately compute all the knowledge in the world of how people live." We stared at him, like we always did. "That alien would be like, 'It seems pretty strange to me that employers have all the power here and employees do what they say. Why would people do that? Who are these great big employees? Why would anyone submit to this kind of a life?'"

Pat always got his share of strange looks when offering this kind of analysis. But you had to hand it to the guy, he was genuine. And the customer invariably gets it. We're offering a win-win for both employee and employer alike. The worker has more autonomy but—courtesy of the Catalant platform—employers get to harness talent when they need it. "With the technology we've already got," Pat invariably would say to a potential new customer, "How come you need all these employees taking up space in your office, when you can see them over a computer screen wherever and whenever you need them?" Say what you will, Pat's vision was starting to get legs.

CHAPTER **10**

The Rules Do Not Apply

The Disruption was coming. That much we knew. And not just because we were willing the disruption with this platform we were building. It wasn't just us. New technologies that enabled collaboration, sharing, and messaging, for example—unrecognizable from a mere decade ago—were rapidly penetrating the workplace. Our little venture just happened to tap into one vital cog in the wheel, the one that embraced and empowered the flexible workforce. Great idea!

However, being in the right place at the right time was not enough. Old-school companies were locked into ironclad ways of doing business that had barely caught up to the twenty-first century, much less the year 2017. Planning and budgeting, procurement and the legal frameworks that followed, training and the HR function—they all were cloaked in departments that still boasted dated IT and prehistoric databases. If you looked hard under the hood at some of these corporations, you could still find landlines. Printouts. File cabinets! We may have had the ear of some of the great strategists and visionaries of the new age, but checks would be written by hand, not heart. That meant we had to demonstrate that Catalant couldn't just solve your day-to-day problems but change the way you do business.

One of our most sacred internal manifestos we call our Key Account Journey, and it is our fervent belief that if we can convey it to potential customers, we can grow our business and change theirs. There are two big categories that compose our sales philosophy.

One: there must be an up-front commitment from a champion within the company we are helping. This means we need to make a good enough business case to convince the customer to get serious. Otherwise we've given it our best shot but end up with little more than "happy ears"—the polite listen along with that thousand-mile stare that suggests we may hear back from them in a month, or 12.

Second: we need to provide the customer with the logistical underpinnings—the operating framework and the right contracts with the finance and procurement team—so that the customer feels supremely comfortable with the actual checkout process. In fact, we consider this one of the most important value propositions we offer—so they are confident they can "check out" on our platform as easily as any consumer can with one click on Amazon.

These tenets of our key action plan are built on the trust engendered from our first engagement with the customer. Maybe that is a small project we have completed, or perhaps it is just a strong referral that leads to a meeting. Regardless, it requires what we call the "action potential," the spark plug that ignites a new relationship. Which means we want to make sure the action potential is not only a complete grand slam, but opens the door to process change that will lead to a much more robust and sustained engagement for everyone involved.

It all sounded great on paper, and we were finally starting to have some luck getting in the door of the larger companies—the kinds of places we knew could grow our business to the next level. And we were getting good at the pitch. But that didn't necessarily mean that we were always closing the deals we wanted and needed. It brought on a period of soul searching. What could we do better? How could we more efficiently relate to the customer? What was our role in this brave new world, and how could we find ways to mutually help one another?

Rich, our first Head of Sales, had his own take on it. "Organizations just aren't ready for the future of work," he announced one day. "In fact, they are built for an entirely different mission." He was talking about two pillars in the corporate infrastructure, HR and procurement. While more and more companies were starting to think and talk about how to leverage the benefits of the external knowledge pool, there were structural impediments holding back progress. Responsibility for building and managing a contingent knowledge-based worker program typically falls in a gap between a company's procurement and HR teams. At many companies, utilization of the flexible workforce (formerly and often still known as big consulting) falls firmly in procurement's camp. Entrenched providers make their way onto preferred supplier lists, negotiate rate cards, and put master services agreements in place. HR works with legal to manage the procurement relationships, be it consulting or old-school temporary staffing. The problem was, what our platform was bringing to the table was unaffiliated with any of these solutions, so what we were pitching fell outside of the procurement mandate. What's more, HR was predominantly tasked with managing the full-time employee load or contingent blue-collar roles. So yet again, our experts fell beyond the pale of the HR portfolio at most companies. So, if neither procurement nor HR was curating the flexible knowledge-based workforce, who was?

It was a conundrum we were losing sleep over. And if you could somehow tiptoe through this minefield, you had to convince the people in finance that investing a good part of their spend on the on-demand worker was a good idea. That wasn't a shoo-in, either.

Budgets are getting crunched in good times and bad. Cutting costs rewards the financial manager a lot more than finding new ones—no matter if we were a better long-term solution than the excessive consulting burns most companies had been accustomed to for decades. When the bottom line is measured in quarters, it's a tough sell convincing someone that an MBA out in Boulder is going to solve your financial crisis here in New York or Boston or Chicago—in FY2020! Lastly, throw in the obvious complexity around legal—how companies manage opening their doors to outsiders—and you had the perfect storm. We hoped for a much better result.

All of these traditional corporate functions are about risk management, and it's hard for innovation to thrive in an environment where risk does not. And, of course, when you are the new kid on the block, every time you knock on a door, all people tend to see is risk. We were going to have to do something about that.

One thing was vividly clear. Companies can no longer succeed with only a roster of full-time employees. The deficit of high-end talent was becoming front-page news. We were witnessing a paradigm shift. What's more, the talent that was out there was hungry for a whole new way of working. The brave ones had cut out on their own, and our platform was being developed to find them new homes. But even the employees who stayed the course and hung onto their jobs were going to be impacted, because the organizations were catching on, too. We were all going to have to play in the same sandbox. That meant the rules were going to have to change. Some got it.

Although many of our customers are considered visionary product innovators, we often find we need to challenge them to think differently about engaging talent if they are truly going to leverage a resource like ours. For example, if you are part of the strategy team at a leading software firm, odds are that you are trying to assess dozens of new growth opportunities at any given time. You've only got so many people on your team who can only work so many hours a week, and you also only have so many dollars in your budget to hire a consulting firm to fill some of your information gaps. So if you only have a few million in your consulting budget, how do you optimize every dollar of that spend? You could invest the entire sum with a Big Three firm to explore one opportunity, or use the same amount and hire 10 Catalant experts for 10 opportunity assessments.

We were lucky to get an audience with one of the big software firms. They took a shot with us and loved the result. Now they have a different attitude about the work they do through our platform because we had a really useful conversation. And they've calibrated their risk accordingly. That's the kind of creative project scoping and spending we wanted to be discussing with our customers. And it was not just about cheap consulting. Nobody wants cheap sushi. We were always careful to emphasize quality over cost. Fortunately, our enterprise buyers place a similar importance on top-quality work, and our experts were up for the challenge.

On a global scale, the adjustment that some companies made was in their risk-calculation processes. As an organization, if you are committed to leveraging the flexible workforce, then you can't use the same expectations that you might for other on-demand services or a contract with the Big Three. The same risks do not apply. And we happen to believe this is a must-do calculation for any company that is ready for the future of work. They will calibrate to what you can do for them and what the actual work is. Our job was to convince them to throw away the same rubber stamp they've applied in the past. That was not going to work for the companies of today or, for that matter, tomorrow. Our platform was the new kid in town. But was corporate America ready to buy in?

* * *

Organizations that want to stay ahead of the curve are going to have to adapt to a new mind-set if they want to leverage the capabilities of the flexible workforce. The early adopters who signed on with us understood that we were giving them access to an unconstrained workforce. How on Earth were companies—some of them founded decades ago and still rattling those old steel file cabinets—going to roll with the punches?

This was not as simple as creating a new file on an employee. It required a wholesale change in thinking, to adopt processes into the ecosystem of the company.

We were growing comfortable with the fact that our platform was changing the way companies did business. It's been exciting living on the cutting-edge of a new industry. Yet it's also meant an up-close view of the many ways that regulatory policy—the law, and government policies—need to catch up.

In 2015, the U.S. Government Accountability Office (GAO) estimated that 40 percent of the workforce was working a contingent job, whether as a temp, a contract worker, or a freelancer.[1] Two in every five workers. Yet we still rely on a health care system that is largely connected to one's employer. As a result, freelancers must absorb the entire burden for Social Security (FICA) and Medicare (SECA), whereas that's a shared cost for anyone working a full-time job. That is a material responsibility for most anyone trying to navigate these waters on their own. And it is ripe for change.

Similarly the 401(k) is still tied to your employer and massively inconvenient for anyone shifting to independent work. Unemployment benefits, worker safeguards such as the Family Medical Leave Act (more relevant to temps and contract workers than our experts), and other commonly accepted benefits of staying afloat in today's economy are based on the assumption of a traditional employer-employee relationship. That is a system and a mind-set that is going to become as antiquated as punching a timecard. The workforce is demanding it. But even more so, the internal mind-set of HQ is going to have to adapt, too. These old-school expectations were as core to the company's former operating model as providing Internet access and a place to eat your lunch are to today's workers. Lots of minds were going to have to change to integrate and grow the whole new system.

Legal, another building block on the transformation highway, requires a whole different kind of hand-holding. In-house legal

---

[1] www.gao.gov/products/GAO-15-168R.

departments were accustomed to protecting company assets when employees engaged with outside resources at conferences, in a network, or on an airplane. The lawyers were empowered to protect as much of the company's assets as possible, recognizing these kind of exchanges happen every day. We had that covered. Having a platform like ours gives a legal team the ability to track which consultants worked on which projects. In fact, our platform was more trackable than the wayward employee working on his laptop over his third cocktail at the Ambassador Lounge. There was no tracking that. Our platform allowed for a lot more accountability.

To help us navigate these corporate legal departments, we hired Shirley Paley as general counsel at the end of 2016. Shirley had most recently been negotiating SaaS customer contracts with Demandware which was acquired by Salesforce and had the stellar background we sought, including seven years with law firm Goodwin Procter and outstanding academic credentials. Shirley devotes much of her time to negotiations with our most sophisticated customers.

The C-suite also needs to catch up. Organizations need to rewrite policies and procedures to more smoothly integrate independent workers. Planning and budgeting need to change, as well as procurement and HR. Training across the spectrum needs to be revamped. The days of one-size-fits-all ended long ago—and it's incumbent on the HR department to drive this change. But when we were fortunate to get an audience with the game changers, how could we make a dent?

All of these executive management fronts were part of the equation we were trying to sell, and it was no easy task, that was for sure. In order to be heard, we tried to meet with the VP or SVP who had a budget to manage and, coincidentally, a career to run. No matter the changes afoot, people are still incentivized by success, and we wanted the ears of people who want to look good for the company and good for themselves. When we got in that door, we positioned our platform as an innovative tool that can help them with their career trajectory. It took some explaining. We had to demonstrate that it's the platform more than the expert. The expert is under the hood. We explained that you are buying a utility that has value beyond any single individual expert. If you are focused on budget, for that $10 million of spend you can get $14 million of return on investment (ROI). How could anyone say no to that? We saw it as an overlap between managers' personal and professional goals, one that would have a really practical impact on their budgets and their teams' bandwidth. Basically, we had to relay what we knew and believed: choose us and you are an innovator unlocking a tool that will have value beyond your own team.

Once we got traction in these conversations, we tried to seek a master agreement with the enterprise to engage any user anywhere in their company. That did not always come easily. On our non-enterprise contracts, a typical project timeframe is four to six weeks. That was great for revenue, but not so strategic in the long run. A project without an enterprise agreement was a means to an end: get enough projects to trigger the enterprise process and you had something.

Another piece in our strategic thinking was an eye toward partnerships as a way to grow our business. Many of the large enterprises we sought had long-standing contracts with partners for staffing and contingent talent, as well as vendor management and software systems management. It all worked hand in hand, and entrenched players were incentivized to control the outside spend. What if we could partner with some of these providers, say, for example, a Kelly Services? There is no resource for engaging high-end business talent on demand like we have. Managed service providers (MSPs) see the flexible workforce as a gap in the talent supply chain that they are filling for customers. And VMSs (software) see it as a way to capture really big project spends in their systems. Hand in hand, couldn't we all partner to optimize the flexible workforce of the company of the future?

* * *

In all these cases where old dogs needed to learn new tricks, the old system was predicated on mitigating risk. But we were proposing a whole new way of thinking that did not necessarily play into the risk mitigation model. So once we got in front of a customer, what was that manager supposed to do? And how could we convince him to do it?

It's our belief that flexibility and speed are two of the key ingredients for change. Be ready to try one thing, and if that doesn't work, adapt, and adapt quickly. It may not eliminate risk, but it minimizes it. If your company is nimble, you are likely to benefit from the changes that are overtaking the workplace, and when a model needs some retooling, you are nimble to do that, too. The flexible workforce model comes in many sizes. Contracts have to reflect the diversity and geography of your new workers. Payment policies can be as wide-ranging as the needs of the people you are paying. The numbers still matter. Cost-effectiveness counts. But how you choose to craft your finances can be as flexible as the people you are paying.

Even training will come under the umbrella of change as this generation evolves. Figuring out the best resources to deploy for an in-house deliverable will be a key component of the new manager's job. The company that puts in place training policies for its layers of management will adapt more quickly, again cutting out a layer of risk from the process. The new HR department will hone its strategies around a mix of internal and external capabilities. They will be tasked with contracting and managing a far-flung network of integrated contributors. Top-drawer HR managers will not just manage people; they will curate the whole ecosystem.

We were building our platform to meet the needs of companies and the on-demand workforce that they would need to remain competitive in this changing world. But companies were going to have to do more than sign up for this to work for everyone. The case studies we were seeing that worked had put new processes and procedures into place that changed the whole picture. First and foremost, we found that if there was one influencer who embraced the change at the most foundational level, then others would follow. It is hard to inspire managers across an organization unless there is one strong advocate who truly gets onboard. That was the person we sought out when we were making our deals.

When that leader took the initiative to shake things up, it usually involved a series of changes that may have looked foreign to management at first, but in fact facilitated the process of transformation. This stuff wasn't happening by accident. There were protocols in place and documentation. Teams had to grow, and deliverables were tested and benchmarked. Management needed to know what worked and what didn't. Our platform had built-in technologies to aid and abet the cause, but humans were still needed to keep the machine well-oiled and running. Success is measured not just in cost savings but in behavioral change as well. We were just the instrument of change. Leadership had to adopt what we were selling or there might be strife on the factory floor, so to speak.

People are not always receptive to change. We spend a lot of time in our internal meetings asking if we were disrupters or enablers. Could you be both and bring about positive change for all involved? From our perspective, the traditional corporate org chart has grown stale and dated, and as a result, business growth has become narrow and limited. It is hardly a hotbed for innovation if you are operating with the engine of a 2004 gas-guzzler. Furthermore, it was becoming more and more evident in the new tech economy that there simply were not enough skilled workers to go around. And if you thought you'd be able to cherry-pick them with the old manual systems (Help Wanted ads, anyone?), or even the new-age tools, like Monster or LinkedIn, you were still operating behind the curve. It was not enough to think you could populate a forward-thinking company from backward-thinking channels. The system would not withstand the pressure.

The smart companies, we were learning from the evidence of our platform data, were becoming agile outside their own walls. They were integrating external and internal head count to maximize their ability to deliver. Their new HR people were learning the ropes of the on-demand workforce in order to offer best practices and human lifestyle solutions to the people who were going to be their new most valuable resources. With speed and agility, risk became less. And with flexibility, your strategic options were going to multiply.

As Pat explained, we were rebuilding our platform and coming up with new contracts to manage different pools of talent. "It's all just a bridge to get to what the future of work actually looks like," he said. "It will help customers become agnostic, which is the gateway to the future of work."

CHAPTER 11

Fake It 'til You Make It

Fall 2015–Spring 2016

In a conversation with an executive with a large company that had just started using our platform, we asked a simple question. How much do you figure your company spends on consulting each year? Little did we know that our casual query would point the way to another critical tool destined to help liberate all those businesses and employees eager to find a better, more sensible way of thinking about work.

The executive confessed he had no idea. But apparently we had piqued his interest. Just our asking the question made him determined to find out.

One week passed, then another. Finally, he got back to us with an answer. "Around $500 million?" Seemed fair. But then a week later, he was back in touch again. "Actually, we just found another $120 million in costs." Hmmm, we thought. So he'd underestimated by more than 25 percent. We'd have been out of business a long time ago if our math was that bad. Turns out, our friend was not done. Clearly we had unleashed the monster within. We received several more updates over the coming weeks. They had found another $50 million here and another $50 million there. Then he got back to us with this. "Hey guys," he said brightly. "Turns out that we don't really track anything under $200,000. So all the numbers we've given you so far are just for projects that cost more than that."

Once we were done digesting this valuable kernel of data, we tried to figure out what to make of it. We thought maybe this company was an outlier. But as we made progress among our growing roster of enterprise customers, we had the chance to ask others the same question, and we were finding that the answers were markedly similar. The managers tasked with counting the dimes and nickels had no idea what their company spent on consulting. Like so many large organizations, they figured that finding out was as simple as calling someone over in finance. But the harder they dug, the more empty-handed they came up. Finding anything like a hard dollar figure proved elusive. It seemed no company had found an adequate method for tracking their consulting spend. The most sophisticated system we came across was one corporate giant that at least had someone on payroll whose job it was to enter the consultant spend in an Excel spreadsheet each month. We confess to being a bit slack-jawed at this news, as if someone had let us in on a company secret, only we weren't quite sure what to do with it.

A lack of financial accounting was only part of the problem. The large corporate behemoths were spending hundreds of millions of dollars a year on consultants, and yet there was no central repository of the reports and collateral materials they produced. Could this really be? We heard anecdote after anecdote that left us shaking our heads. One company had paid a consulting firm somewhere around $5 million, but the top executive who initially sponsored the project had left the company and no one knew what might have happened to the final report. To us, this would be like a logistics company sending out several dozen tractor trailers full of goods that never turned up anywhere. Like the Bermuda triangle of freight. Gone, without so much as a pencil scratch on a ledger sheet.

The most common affliction we could perceive inside the large enterprise seemed to be redundancy. A company would write a seven-figure check to study a market or strategy and have no idea that their counterpart down the hall had paid for that same deliverable 12 months earlier. One division head inside a global giant told us he figured his unit alone wasted $10 million a year on redundant spend, commissioning projects for which the company already knew the answer. If only they knew where to find the study. The problem, as hard as we found it to believe, was that there was no centralized accounting for the work done by people outside the company—or for large projects done by teams within the enterprise, for that matter. We were reminded of the old sci-fi adage, "If you scream in space, will anyone hear your cry?"

Out of this reckless management accounting came our brainstorm for an enterprise-grade software package that could help large enterprise companies keep track of all of their deliverables, whether a project was handled in-house, by someone working through our platform, or by the universe of outside consulting firms they used. Our solution would live online on their own business Intranet and give executives a better, more intelligible view of projects completed, as well as projects in the works. We would make it easily searchable so that a prior consulting spend wasn't wasted money. Then we would add the analytic tools to help them better manage that spend over time.

We'd also add a Yelp-like review feature that allowed people within the company to evaluate and rate their experience with various vendors. That was something else we had learned talking with people inside the enterprise: a division head might have had a horrible experience working with a big consulting outfit, but there was no easy way to disseminate that information among colleagues, short of a random email blast. This seemed positively prehistoric to us. You drop a few million dollars on a job, the project comes out a flop, and it's on you to shoot off an email while you're picking up dinner at local supermarket Wegman's? There had to be a better way. We proposed a single knowledge database that a company could access to track and archive any deliverable, and then scour them via tags and robust search tools.

There was, however, one potential issue with our grandiose scheme, and it was a technical one. The original HourlyNerd was a marketplace, not a software shop. What we were proposing would put us in the software-as-a-service business, like Salesforce or NetSuite. But Brian Morgan, our CTO, assured us it was doable. Already his team was building tools and analytics to help both customers and Nerds get more out of our platform. All he needed was the budget to bring on more programmers.

The lingering question was whether anyone would have any interest in buying the product we had in mind. We might have been blown away that businesses had such a poor a handle on their consulting spend. And we found it unfathomable that they had no system to track their results. But they'd come this far down the road without anyone even noticing that the trunk was wide open and the contents were spilling out all over the highway. Would our target market care enough about the problem to actually spend money on a fix?

* * *

We were not hosting an enterprise-ready product website at the start of 2014 when we did our first big enterprise deals. But we knew that business signaled both the start of something big and a new challenge that we would have to address. Brian was building up the back end and pushing toward a completely web-based user interface. By early 2015, we were already offering a white-label capability so that an enterprise could create its own private, secured version of our site. GE, for instance, created its own ge.hourlynerd.com portal, open only to project buyers with a GE email and those select experts invited to bid on GE's projects.

Pat suggested we apply our usual "ask and scope" approach to test the market for a broader enterprise software. "Why don't we pretend it's a real website," he said, "and show it to our customers to see what they think?" We had a big presentation coming up with a Fortune 100 company. We all agreed it was worth a test, so that weekend Pat had a designer create a dozen slides that looked like pages from the site we hoped to develop. He then threw it into InVision, an app that creates more realistic-looking prototypes. We were ready to go.

The meeting was basically a Q&A session about our SMB platform. The company that had invited us to present wanted to learn more about the start-up scene and the small- and medium-sized businesses that used us and why. Pat ran through his usual shoot-from-the-hip dog-and-pony show, mixing in his exuberant enthusiasm with a more than ample diet of useful information. When he was done with his presentation, he asked if anyone wanted to look at an enterprise solution that we'd been working on. They of course said yes.

Pat had prepared and practiced for this moment. He had made sure that the URL on the slides—an InVision address that would be a dead tell for an early stage prototype —was out of sight. The prototype was clickable and our cover was safe, so long as he knew exactly where to click. "You can hire Bain through this site," he told the 40 or so people in the room. "You can form teams of people. You can do analytics on all your consulting spend. You can capture all the deliverables." He made sure to click through as quickly as possible so no one in the room could stop to look too hard or ask questions. They could see that the site would show the status of a project, the point person inside the company for each, or the price parameters. But that's as far as his presentation went. If there was so much as a single question, Pat couldn't close a dialogue box, open a new page, or have a deeper look at drop-down menus and the other bells and whistles analysts liked to see. Thank goodness Pat was a quick and compelling speaker. The screen had already faded to black when he asked, "What do you think?"

"Can we meet next week about it?" We all breathed a sigh of relief.

Our confidence bolstered, our impromptu website and slide deck would make a cameo a few weeks later when Pat and Pat Mascia, who was running the industrial vertical for us, were in Los Angeles to meet with a different Fortune 100 company. "Can you show us the platform?" they asked. They didn't mean the normal HourlyNerd marketplace, but one that included all these other elements we imagined layering on top—the ones we had been talking up for the previous 20 minutes.

Once again, we walked them through our prototype as fast as we could. Only this time, someone hit the pause button on Pat. "Can you go back so we can take a deeper look at that page?"

"Ahhh, sorry, but the Internet in this Starbucks is really lousy," Pat told them. Never had we been so happy to present our show in a coffee shop. Our daring had landed us a second large enterprise eager to hear about our theoretical new software package, and all it cost us was a few hundred man-hours and a half dozen venti macchiatos.

* * *

We spent a lot of time debating what to do in the coming weeks. Customers seemed to like this idea of software that would provide them with a 360-degree view of their consultant spend and let them better manage their expertise. Polling showed that 34 percent of all businesses were dissatisfied with the rigmarole of dealing with consultants and other outside experts. Twice that many (68 percent) expressed a "strong" or "very strong" interest in a tool that would enable easier and quicker hiring and onboarding of outside talent.

But adding that kind of sophisticated capabilities to our two-sided marketplace represented a huge departure. We were a transactional site talking about morphing into a knowledge base to help an enterprise track, analyze, and archive the sum total of its deliverables, whether in the hands of people inside the company or outside, or a combination of the two. We needed to consider the ramifications of so profound a shift in strategy. There seemed to be a business there—but was it the one we should be pursuing in the fall of 2015?

We had taken a big step when we repositioned the company to focus more heavily on enterprise customers. As it was, we were still in hiring mode to build out our enterprise sales team. And here we were contemplating another overhaul in our business model. We were already creating one market from scratch; another zigzag like that would mean creating a second. Complicating the decision, software as a service was its own unique galaxy that demanded specialized sales expertise. Our people were just learning how to convince big companies to post projects on our site. They were getting good at selling consulting projects. Could we also ask them to transform themselves into software salespeople?

Pat harbored no doubts about what we should do. Invariably, he was the first on board with any new idea, no matter how crazy or improbable it might seem. He pointed out that we wouldn't be diving into this without first doing our homework. He had prototyped what we had in mind. We had tested it among customers, albeit a few. We were already gathering feedback on ways to improve the product. To Pat, we had all the proof points we needed.

Peter, our CFO, was the most conservative of the gang, and there was probably some real wisdom and luck in that. It's the chief financial officer's job to manage the financial risks of a company. The CFO is also in charge of financial planning. Our revenues were growing at a rapid pace, as were our margins. And the dramatic pivot we were considering threatened to knock us off our enviable growth curve. Peter started computing in his head the dollars required to get us to where we needed to be. As it was, we were spending more than we were earning in pursuit of the opportunity to land all those large enterprises we imagined posting projects in our marketplace. That initiative had begun in earnest less than a year ago. And now here we were considering an even more ambitious retooling of the company.

As CFO, Peter understood the value proposition of what we were offering. A company's consulting and outside advisor spend is typically opaque and may be the least understood line on an income statement. What is the return on investment of a consulting spend? Why this vendor over that one? Did you actually solve a problem, or just create new ones with all that spending? We were finally overcoming the hurdle of answering those questions for the people who had to green-light the spend on us, and now we were asking them to mix it all up? Ours was still a modest-sized start-up, already stretched thin by the scale of our ambition. "We simply don't have the resources to develop two products at once," Peter said and then in the same breath asked, "How are we going to do this?"

Rob's views were, per usual, balanced. We were a marketplace, not a software shop, he said. True enterprise software wasn't, at that point, in the company DNA. He saw the risk in changing direction and disrupting the existing business we were building. The model was working, whereas pursuing this new vision would require developing new muscles and shifting our burn rate into overdrive. We'd need to supersize the tech team and also expand sales. That would mean raising more money well ahead of schedule, which could prove another huge distraction. When the three of us were in fund-raising mode, it tended to eat up 8 or 10 hours of every day. And who knew how the venture market would respond if we went back out seeking more capital after so recently closing on our previous round of financing? We'd had an incredible run at the table. Sometimes you have to know when to pocket a few chips.

Rob also pointed out the long-term challenge in developing and pushing a product we hadn't proved the market wanted. Yes, a couple of large companies had expressed interest. And, yes, the product made perfect commercial sense. But could we really fundamentally change the way business bought consulting services?

But Rob was also a risk taker at heart. In football terms, he believed in the ground game and short passes, but he also believed that over the course of building a truly disruptive start-up there would be a precious few ideal moments to rear back and throw the ball all the way to the end zone. And this seemed a moment for airing it out. He had read many corporate histories where one key aggressive decision had made all the difference. We could stick to the path we set, and if everything went right, he saw it, we could build a company worth a few hundred million dollars. But successfully opening up this new market had the potential to transform us into a world-changing company. We could define the future of work, with our procurement and consulting software-as-a-service (SaaS) serving as the tip of the spear. It was a classic choice between the safe choice and a high-risk, high-reward alternative—with Rob and Pat clearly in favor of taking the gamble. Paraphrasing *Risky Business*, "Sometimes you gotta say, what the [hell]."

We all recognized this as one of those bet-the-company decisions we'd read about seemingly ages ago in our HBS case studies. But in this case, it seemed worth it. The SaaS strategy, if successful, would mean a stable stream of recurring revenue at much higher gross margins than those of any gig posted on our marketplace. There was also the potential for increased spend on our platform with any company choosing to license our software—people almost by definition interested in better managing their consulting costs. And, of course, by giving executives a dashboard that allows them to more easily and effectively manage their outside spend, we were enabling the project-based view of work we were promoting.

After a lot of soul searching, it became apparent to us that we were trying to become more than just another solution provider you use to solve a few problems every quarter. We saw ourselves as becoming **the** operating system through which an enterprise manages the future of its human capital. And the only way to do that would be to pursue this software play. Which meant we needed to make the requisite investments.

The good news was that we had come to a decision. That was also the bad news, too, because once again we'd need to gear up for a fund-raising drive. With potential investors again poring over our books that meant pushing our people to scrape and crawl for every dollar. We grew our bookings by 29 percent between the third and fourth quarters of 2015 and pushed them up another 53 percent in the first quarter of 2016. We calculated that we'd need two to four years of cash runway to pull off our SaaS strategy. We figured it would take that long before we saw any meaningful software licensing fees.

Based on our phenomenal traction and a broader future vision, we were able to raise $22 million in Series C funding. Highland Capital again invested in the company, along with GE Ventures and Bob Doris. But this time, General Catalyst in Cambridge led the financing. We first met General Catalyst co-founder David Fialkow back in 2013. He's been a strong champion for us along the way. "Catalant is going to fundamentally change how work happens, so we were psyched that we built a strong relationship with the team and had the opportunity to support them on their journey," he said. We were just glad that we had one of venture's most amazing firms in our corner. GC's list of hits includes Kayak, HubSpot, Stripe, Warby Parker, and Airbnb, among others. Not bad company to be in!

Since meeting David, even before he invested, he has been an incredible source of guidance, mentorship, and direction for us—often jumping on calls late at night or very early in the morning. We feel lucky to have been continuously supported by the some of the best few people in the VC industry; our time working with GC officially since March of 2016 has been exciting, rewarding, and memorable.

Mark Cuban was also among those choosing to invest again in the Series C. We had disappointed Mark in the early days of the company with slow growth and therefore were gratified that he chose to back us financially. But more than money, it was Mark's words that left us speechless. "In the same way that Amazon Web Services re-defined how companies think about technology," he said in a press statement, "HourlyNerd is redefining how companies engage top talent."

CHAPTER 12

Win with Technology

2016

Large enterprises are looking for a competitive edge in today's increasingly competitive labor market. Catalant enables top companies to find top talent quickly and cost effectively.

—CRAIG DRISCOLL, HIGHLAND CAPITAL

Mark Cuban was right, of course: at its core, our platform was about connecting businesses to elite talent. Companies expressed the problem in different ways. They would talk about a "talent gap" or express frustrations they felt attracting the right people—the best people—to their company. The workload varied, but their ability to add capacity was rigid. Those in management positions felt enormous stress struggling to meet their goals through maternity and sick leave or a seasonal crunch. Some expressed a frustration that came down to this: their company had tens of thousands of people in their employee base and yet they often didn't have the people they needed to get the basic work done—and that was hurting business. For many, the reality was that specialization was more critical than ever. However, the answer wasn't to add to the head count but to make sure they had access to the right person at the right moment.

No matter how they expressed it, the pain point was always the same: there is something broken in the workplace. Companies were in desperate need of help. Technology had the potential to cause a seismic shift in how business got things done. They could use a platform like ours to locate and engage happier, more focused workers. Now the challenge was to convince business leaders that we were offering a solution to much of what ailed them.

❋ ❋ ❋

We figured private equity would be open to trying our platform. Historically they have been big buyers of high-priced consulting talents, and they thought of the world in terms of projects and opportunities. By nature, private equity seeks to squeeze costs and seize on efficiencies when they present themselves. There would be no great need to educate them about the future of work. At the start of 2016, we launched a sales team to pursue large companies in financial, business, and legal services. They would start with private equity and then work at selling our platform to the broader world of finance and also the legal community, which were also large consumers of consulting services.

Our thesis about private equity was borne out. Within six months of launching our new pod, we had more than 80 firms using the platform. Our momentum freed that pod to start knocking on the doors of the big banks and other large financial firms. We were able to gain some traction there, too. Two Boston-based giants of the investment management world were starting to post projects on our site. But selling into larger financial institutions generally means dealing with more hierarchies and red tape. There's a lot more education involved trying to convince an old-school established enterprise to give us a try, or as we like to say, to take "the buyer's journey."

Chris Collins, one of our general managers (GMs), oversees our tech group. One might assume that selling to some of the globe's most innovative companies means Chris has an easier job than the other GMs at our company. But one of life's ironies is that companies that are the most disruptive are also most resistant to the vision we were selling, partially because they typically had far better access to talent than some of our more staid manufacturing clients.

But Chris was a seasoned salesperson whose resume also included stints as a consultant at IBM, MonitorDeloitte, and the Yankee Group (a well-regarded tech consulting group based in Boston). "You need to find a way to tell a story that is compelling enough that companies want to revisit an area they see as scary," he said. "You convince a company to post a small project to the site, delight them with the results, and then convince them next time to use us to solve a bigger, more ambitious project." He used the same lines that all of us used. Only the best people can go into business for themselves and succeed. Do the math: you get quality at considerable savings.

Pat Griffin was the GM in charge of retail and consumer packaged goods, which is basically anything sold in a store. Pat G. would secure a big win shortly after starting in mid-2015 when he convinced the head of strategy and finance at one of the world's larger restaurant companies to post a project. "I never respond to this kind of outreach," the woman told him—but she was also tired of spilling millions enlisting consultants to produce a product that left her unsatisfied. We signed the company up for a six-month, $120,000 project completed by a 28-year-old consultant. The client was pleased and would turn to us when looking for a new tech system to improve functionality through the chain. They didn't need to spend $1 million to figure it out. They had a strong internal team. They only needed an outsider to go out and do some due diligence on their behalf. We were really showing our chops.

Yet retail and CPG were also proving a tough sell. People got it. They understood it would save them money. They understood that it gave them access to a wider pool of talent outside of their usual networks. But packaged goods and retail occupied generally cautious corners of the economy. Few want to be pioneers, and they need a lot of assurances. Pat G. was able to assuage the worries of the person he was talking with by stressing the quality of our experts and noting that ours is a twenty-first-century way of finding talent. But there's always the question of how much power the people he speaks to actually have. "There's all these off-stage players that need convincing—procurement, legal, HR—but it's not like you get to have conversations with them," Pat G. said. Among the phrases he hears a lot: "Let me get back to you."

Nick Blum would take over health care a few months into 2016. Prior to coming to work for us, Nick headed the San Francisco office for Applied Predictive Technologies, a software company in the data analytics business. Prior to that, Nick worked as a management consultant specifically focused on the life sciences. One challenge of selling into big pharma and the major biotech companies, which are some of the biggest spenders on traditional consulting, is that the upside of a blockbuster drug tends to outweigh price sensitivity around professional services. Moreover, life sciences companies generally tend to be more risk averse, given their stakes in caring for people's lives.

Still, Nick figured out that the generic drug manufacturers and medical device makers both tended to be located in less desirable parts of the country and therefore faced the greatest immediate talent crunch. Nick and his team would make progress among that category of companies, as well as among the pre-commercial biotech industry. These latter companies were typically businesses being run fairly lean as they awaited favorable FDA trial results—companies invariably with deep scientific rosters but usually thin on commercial talent. Among the companies he had signed up in this category was an innovative medical device maker that had just secured phase three approval. They needed help in almost every part of their commercial organization, from pricing to sales to marketing.

"You get good trial results but it's not like you can just go to the open market and yell, 'All right marketers, alright sales, let's build out the commercial capability,'" Nick said. "So we serve as the stop-gap to their ramping up that function. And once we get inside, we help them understand they may not need as big a head count as they thought because we can be a resource to help them when they need it. So much of the work required to commercialize drugs and devices is cyclical, and therefore better suited to on-demand talent solutions than an army of FTEs."

Nick would also inherit our budding relationship with a critical life sciences company when he took over the health care vertical. It would take some work, but ultimately we were able to convince the Fortune 50 company that Catalant should be a source of leverage for teams across their organization.

"It's a process gaining the trust of a critical life sciences company but the good part is once you're in, you're in, then they start to realize the value of our model," Nick said. "We have a tremendous opportunity to replace some of their traditional consulting spend with more targeted and cost-effective solutions. Given the size of the category, there is significant upside for Catalant." Another benefit is clearing their lengthy approval process in order to gain a spot on the approved vendor list. It got us in the door and set up a barrier for any competitor who wants to follow behind us. More importantly, it offered the client a one-stop shop for talent of all types without the hassle of renegotiating terms each time.

❊ ❊ ❊

We changed the name of the company in 2016. The three of us loved the HourlyNerd moniker, but it was also proving something of an albatross among potential customers, especially as we were moving upmarket and selling to larger companies. Our sales-people would make a call and potential customers would say, "We don't need the Geek Squad." The name also caused some to ques-tion the quality of our experts or, worse, viewed the name as a deal killer. The more honest among our target customers would tell salespeople, "I'm gonna tell my boss that I hired some company called HourlyNerd to solve this problem for me? Screw that."

We became Catalant Technologies—a combination of catalyst and talent, with a bit of brilliant tossed in. We also added a new tagline: *Accomplish More*. In the press statement we sent out not-ing the name change, Pat explained: "We are rapidly defining a new market category, and we need to create a brand identity that speaks to this evolution." We would keep the HourlyNerd web-site for small businesses, but now under the name "HourlyNerd powered by Catalant." Like it or not, we were starting to become grown-ups.

We also changed our marketing message as we morphed into a company focused more on enterprise customers. The message in 2015 had been around this idea that we were disrupting the con-sulting world. At that point, we were still focused on the project buyers and the notion they could save money while gaining access to top talent. ("Consulting. On your terms.") The pain point we were rubbing up against was that they were spending so much for outside help and getting suboptimal results.

The new message focused on the C-suite and other top decision makers—those our salespeople were having a hard time reaching more directly. This pitch was much broader than the disruption of the consulting business; it played to a worry that the workforce landscape was changing, but their company wasn't evolving. We chose digital ads aimed at those at director level and above, working within specific industries. We also bought billboards and bus shelter ads along routes we knew would be traveled by our target audience. "Stretched too thin?" one asked.

Another read, "Too many projects? Too little time?" A third asked: "Need instant leverage?" Each included our logo and offered the same answer. "40,000 Business Experts. On Demand."

The faster we grew, the more critical it became that we tend to the ecosystem of our marketplace. We didn't have to spend marketing dollars to draw experts to our site because we were adding another 300 to 500 a week. That was causing problems on both the supply and demand side of the equation. We were hearing from people telling us they had put in 5 or 10 years at McKinsey, served as CFO for an established company, or guest lectured at the Harvard Business School—and yet, despite bidding on 15 projects, they had gotten not so much as a single interview. We were hearing as well from people on the demand side who felt overwhelmed by the oversupply of choices.

In the fall of 2015, we hired Andrea Black to serve as director of supply. Andrea, who had earned her MBA from the Tuck School of Business at Dartmouth, had previously served as head of marketing at Joss & Main, the online furniture retailer. We hadn't given Andrea marching orders so much as laid out our problem. We had this invaluable asset called our experts, and basically we needed someone to manage our relationship with them. Her job: do what she could to keep them both busy and happy. Adding to Andrea's challenge was that she would have to make do with a staff of two. Sales was still a higher priority, given our assumption that adding more projects to the site was the single best thing we could do for our experts.

Community would be one watchword under Andrea. Prior to her arrival, we had a short FAQ page for those signing up as experts. That was replaced with a more user-friendly handbook meant as a quick guide for new experts looking for success on the site: how it works, suggestions for building out your profile, advice for engaging with clients. Already we helped our experts with pesky administrative details like billing and collecting.

But Andrea and her team would create content on the site to make Catalant more indispensable to experts—a kind of one-stop shop for the aspiring independent. We added tools to help people build their own website and offered tips on marketing. We also started arranging partnerships with third parties in the business of helping small businesses. "The idea was that you can come to us and say, 'Okay, these are the health care companies I use. These are the companies that I can go to and set up a 401(k). These are the invoicing tools and marketing tools I need to be successful.'" Somehow, without spreading ourselves too thin, we were finding ways to appeal to a very wide range of problems experts might encounter, and as a result, we were becoming as valuable to them as they were to us.

"Win with technology" was one of the "pillars" we coined when we asked the staff to articulate the core tenets of the company. Initially, the wannabe expert only needed an email address from a top-flight business school to sign up for our site. But then we started hearing from people like the HBS alumnus who reached out to tell us that he didn't have an alumni email address because he had graduated in 1976. We had opened up the site to PhDs, MDs, and others with business skills relevant to our clients, but we also needed some kind of screening to measure for quality. So Andrea, working with our tech team, helped develop an algorithm that analyzes resumes first to determine access to the site and then rates business expertise. Consultants are scored on a scale of one to five, which helps identify top tier quality on behalf of customers and also determines which experts receive access to what projects.

Hers was a department of three, but Andrea would add a concierge element to the relationship mix. She created an email address for any expert wanting to reach someone on her team, and a dedicated phone line for those wanting to talk with an actual human. Each week Andrea and the people on her team proactively phoned a sampling of the fours and fives from the ratings scorecards—to get a better sense of who they were and how they found the site. She also wanted to offer her small department up as a resource. Feedback is critical to helping us grow and improve the platform. Among the problems she has been working on with our tech and product groups: the bias in favor of those who have already successfully established themselves on the platform.

"If you're a client looking at a profile, it's easy to say, 'Well, this person has 15 recommendations and this person hasn't won a project. We know who we're going with.' We needed to make sure that we're getting new people to start winning more often." Sometimes we needed to put a finger on the scale and push people with the requisite expertise and experience. In the past, we encouraged someone to bid on a project but then they'd learn via an email they weren't chosen. Under Andrea, we turned that process on its head. Technology calls an expert's attention to a relevant project, but it's one of our people—a human being—who lets them know if they weren't chosen and why. The human touch helps soften the disappointment of losing out on a project and is also meant to encourage them to keep trying.

Newcomers on the supply side often assume a race-to-the-bottom element to the site. Yet relevant experience is the most important thing to our typical customers, not price. We rarely see price as a key driver in the ultimate selection. There's also plenty of upselling once an expert engages with the customer. That's among the most powerful messages Andrea's team delivers. It's amazing how often one of our people will get on the phone to scope an assignment—and based on similar experiences with a dozen prior clients, the $50,000 project becomes one worth $100,000.

❖ ❖ ❖

These days, we're up over 40,000[1] experts, as well as thousands of boutique firms who've registered to win their work via the site. We consider that one of our strengths, but key to benefitting from that scale is providing a truly curated experience. We do the lion's share of this using technology, but if ever a customer feels overwhelmed by the complexity of too many choices, our client strategy team is there to help. The ultimate aim is a fully automatic system, but that's a long process of continuously working to refine the variable predictive of making the perfect match. That's another challenge we've thrown at our tech team. Working with Andrea and others, they're creating the algorithms that continue to insert machine learning and algorithms based on each user action taken in the application.

"Surprise and delight" is another of our employee-inspired pillars. A business makes no commitment when it posts a project on the site. There's no obligation to choose any of our experts for whatever the reason. But our job is to make sure they do. Our goal is to ensure that the client is blown away by the quality of consultants they find on our network, and also the speed with which they're able to engage them. And if ever there's a problem (this happens incredibly rarely), we engage Andrea's team, client strategy, and others in a recovery operation. These circumstances actually provide another opportunity to "delight" all involved by making sure that everyone walks away from a negative situation feeling they've been treated fairly.

❄ ❄ ❄

We were well over 100 employees by the end of 2016 and still expanding. The more we grew, the more important the issue of culture. That seemed especially important to the heavy users of our platform. The less centralized the workforce, the more essential to

---

[1] As of August 2017.

cultivate a sense of belonging and stress the benefits of working at Catalant.

As in the early days, we expected people to work hard, but we also didn't expect them to live at the office. We give people the day off during every single calendar holiday because we think they need to go hiking, or go furniture shopping, or take their kids outside. Those who deal with clients on weekends can write back if they have an urgent issue. In crunch times, the engineers are probably logging 70 to 80 hours a week. If the site goes down on a Sunday, they're working. Still, people need a chance to recharge, even if we're a start-up. We largely scale back our activities for the last week of August and over the holidays, when people aren't likely to purchase many consulting projects. Recharging is important.

One thing we all try to do as founders is have a little one-on-one time with new employees that we wouldn't otherwise encounter in the office. We have team lunches and a Friday afternoon guacamole party two or three times a month. At the end of each quarter, we collectively host the company at our homes for dinner. We could emulate certain other venture-backed start-ups and take everyone out to a pricey restaurant, but the bill would be in the many thousands of dollars, and how intimate can a dinner be if attended by a hundred people? Instead, we play host at our individual homes. We break the company into cross groups, order takeout,[2] and then all meet afterwards at a central spot. Brian Morgan, our CTO, who has worked for four prior start-ups, assures us that people see prudence and value as sensible rather than stingy.

To keep the corporate lines of communication open, we created an All-In Committee populated by volunteers from different parts of the company. They work with our new head of people growth, Michele Spitzer, on places where there seems a

---

[2]Rob cooks.

real disconnect between where folks think Catalant should be and where it is today. Every Monday morning, we hold our weekly team meeting. Those who can't attend in person call in to listen. Pat usually starts the meeting in his understated way—pounding the table and yelling, "Let's f--- go!!!"

Amy Villeneuve, a regular at these meetings since she started as an advisor for the company, initially didn't know what to think. A former vice president at Amazon who had run its automation unit, Kiva Systems (later renamed Amazon Robotics), Amy initially cringed every time Pat dropped an F-bomb. But eventually she came around, telling us, "It's appropriate. We're in this battle. And we've got to fight to make sure we execute as best we know how." There's a lot of laughter at these meetings, and yet at the same time it's a chance for people to hear what's going on in other parts of the organization and drive home a message when necessary.

In July of 2016, we hired Brian Kalma as our chief experience officer. Brian had spent eight years in executive roles at Zappos and later Gilt Groupe. Nearly a year passed before Brian even responded to the emails Pat had been sending him—and then, when they finally sat down for coffee, Brian began the conversation by asking, "Why am I even meeting with you?" He gave up a thriving business at a user experience consulting firm to join us, because after an hour with Pat he truly believed we were giving people a different way to engage with the workplace.

Brian would play two general roles inside the company. One was more straightforward. We were imagining our software sitting open on the desktops of managers throughout corporate America—a cockpit view of every project they had in the works—and we were committed to the best possible user experience.

The other role had him thinking about design in a bigger, more holistic way. Since the beginning, our greatest belief was that most workplaces have it wrong: it's not about job retention, but job satisfaction. Brian would imagine ways to foster happier, more productive workers inside Catalant, whether that meant creating stimulating microenvironments within the office or freeing up people to be at their best outside it.

"I had sworn I would never work for first-time founders again," Brian declared. "I said I'd never work in enterprise software and I had sworn off working with consultants. But here I saw a real opportunity to impact society and the way people work." It seemed our message was getting through.

CHAPTER 13

The Future of a Flexible Workforce

2017 and Beyond

In the fall of 2016, human resource leaders from companies around the United States traveled to Boston for a gathering in the Catalant offices. "The Thought Leadership Summit," we called it. From our vantage point, we hoped to hear about strategic initiatives being developed inside organizations that wanted to remain relevant in the 21st century and beyond. The idea was to bring together executives from a dozen or so of the country's most forward-looking companies to talk about trends in the marketplace. We weren't the ones pushing through these macro changes, but we definitely played a key role in enabling them. And for a day-and-a-half we also figured we could serve as catalyst and provocateur. The future of work was happening—and the sheer blind luck of our timing in founding Catalant meant we could play a proactive and positive role among those seeing a better way for both the corporation and the employee.

We conducted an exercise that had people think about what they would do if they could rebuild their company from scratch. (Consensus: far fewer full-time employees.) There were brainstorming sessions on what work needed to remain in the hands of full-time employees and what could be reimagined as project-based. There was a lot of discussion about what people see 5 and 10 years down the road (short answer: a lot more change), and strategies for being prepared for that change (experimentation, an openness to new ideas). For participants, it was a chance to hear from one another, as well as from the experts we had brought in for the event. For us, it was a chance to learn from those on the cutting edge, racing to stay ahead of the curve. It was our opportunity to figure out where we could adjust our product road map accordingly and meet the needs everyone saw coming.

Our friend, Catalant board observer, and management professor from HBS, Joe Fuller, was one of those experts. He got everyone's attention early on with a set of alarming slides pointing to the coming talent crunch. "Management" and "business and financial operations" were two of the fastest-growing employment categories, yet who would fill those positions? Only 33 percent of business leaders polled said college graduates were workforce ready, compared to 96 percent of college administrators who said they were. In short, while the theoretical supply of workers was enormous, the number of workers businesses would want to hire was tiny.

Complicating the picture, Joe said, was the rise of millennials as a force within the workplace. Flexibility, a sense of purpose, societal impact—these were what millennials most care about after salary when considering a job. "Employers must address the dichotomy between a career path and life path. Millennials, who the U.S. Bureau of Labor said will comprise 75 percent of all workers by 2030, want a career that fits into their life and not vice versa. This gives them a lot more bargaining power," Joe said, and it requires businesses to think differently about talent acquisition to compete.

We knew this. We built a business on it. More great ideas and people reside outside the walls of your business than inside, which is why businesses need what Joe called "fluid work arrangements" to thrive.

Rob then delivered his usual "vision for the future of work" presentation about totally dissolving the existing system, resorting to his favorite movie-making imagery to make the point. He chose *Good Will Hunting* as an example because we were in Boston, and what movie says Boston more than the Matt Damon, Ben Affleck, and Robin Williams classic? Miramax made a bundle on *Good Will Hunting*, Rob said, but what if the cast and crew were full-time employees who just sat in the building with each other for 14 years trying to think of good ideas? Talk about inefficient.

"Think of your human resources spend like this," he said. "I have a set of problems and I have a bunch of money to solve those problems, so let me figure out the most efficient way to maximize my talent buy. Internal employees? External?" He declared this breakdown a "ridiculous false distinction" in today's world of the Internet and remote collaboration tools. He criticized all the Future of Work conferences and future-of-work books about equipping leaders with Band-Aids "to make people hate their jobs less."

"We think that in order to have people love what they do, you have to start again with a new paradigm," he said.

For us, the gathering was about learning from a group that deliberately included some participants not yet using Catalant. There were worries about inculcating values among regular freelancers inside mission-driven organizations. People spoke of "blending" (the mixing of full-time, part-time, and independents) as an issue and of the challenges this vision would present to managers, who would need to hone their skills "scoping" projects in the fashion of a Bain consultant. Venturing into the great unknown, how do you model out the costs and structures of this new paradigm? People expressed worry over the loneliness factor among people who worked from home every day. There were concerns about intellectual property protections and data security. There was an acknowledgment that when health care is tied to work, ours is a system structurally biased in favor of full-time employment.

Yet mainly the event seemed a chance for a lot of like-minded people from different industries (tech, pharmaceuticals, industrial) to brainstorm solutions rather than give in to roadblocks. A blended workforce might present a manager with new challenges, but also with new opportunities. A SaaS platform like we were developing lets them access retirees on a project when appropriate, or alumni. Instilling a company's core mission among independent contractors also meant reinforcing an important message among those working within your walls. If much of your team is remote, someone suggested, why not consider biannual meetings that could help with team building, regardless of where someone sat.

One HR executive left a Post-it note on the glass wall of the conference room while we were out to lunch: "Exciting to ponder efficiency gains if we do this right!"

Another participant asked: "Are organizations ready to go truly talent-centric?"

We're happy to leave that question for academics and others studying organizational behavior. But over time, we doubt businesses will have a choice. Every poll we've seen since starting Catalant shows that the talent gap persists as a major pain point for business leaders both in the United States and internationally. A 2016 survey by PricewaterhouseCoopers, for instance, found that 72 percent of chief executives worry about the availability of key skills.

One solution for managers confronting a brain crunch: double down on recruiting efforts. Increase perks and allow for more flexible hours.

Or embrace a future already here for those willing to take advantage of critical tools for any company interested in competing in today's global economy. Look outside those walls. We talk a lot about the high caliber of talent we've attracted to

Catalant since our founding. Simply put, companies won't thrive in today's rapidly changing business environment if they rely on the relatively small number of people who happen to wear that company's employee badge.

Winning organizations put talent front and center. They access, engage, and deploy the best and brightest wherever they can find them. They look to the fixed supply of in-house people they have working for them, but they also search outside for the best talent. It's about getting the work done. As we've learned, the rest figures itself out.

Flexibility, nimbleness, collaboration—those will be the building blocks of success moving forward. Companies that adapt will be able to take advantage of capabilities wherever they are located. They'll plug into what Mark Cuban memorably dubbed the "spot market for intellect," unleashing the fresh energies and thinking of people outside an organization and gaining access to new markets more readily than in the past. They will enjoy newfound agility in seizing strategic opportunities.

We can tell you we're empowering the future of work, but it's not us. It's the technology. Technology lets us easily search talent based on keywords and tags. The genius of the network has opened the doors wide to the finest and most expert talent in the world. We simply provide the match to your company.

Flexible talent-access platforms like ours are empowering this new world of work, making it easier than ever before to bring in the right skills for the right project at the right time. The world's most successful media companies long ago figured out that winning meant finding the right balance between full-timers and freelancers. They saved money while simultaneously ensuring they had access to a wider talent pool.

Digital disruption means that it is incumbent on virtually every company to follow suit. Organizations must be reimagined and rebuilt to catch up. To us, it seems almost existential: the very long-term survival of the corporation requires executives to think about talent in a completely different way.

We've lived through the initial resistance of some businesses to embrace a more fluid view of the people who work for them. Many organizations still look at talent the old-fashioned way: develop a job description, engage in a search, hire for a full-time posting. But old mind-sets and policies that enable an internal-only workforce need to change.

Winning depends on it.

❊ ❊ ❊

Everything we are seeing out on the street and through our own experience points in the direction of the future as we imagine it. On the employer side, our sales pitch and those of others pushing for a rise in the contingent workforce seem to be having an impact. More than 80 percent of the country's large corporations plan to "substantially increase" their use of a flexible workforce in the coming years, according to a 2015 Bureau of Labor Statistics report. At the start of 2016, the World Economic Forum released a report looking at workforce strategies at the start of what the organization dubbed the fourth Industrial Revolution.[1] Of the HR executives surveyed, 44 percent agreed that their "organizations are likely to have an ever-smaller pool of core full-time employees for fixed functions, backed up by colleagues in other countries and external consultants and contractors for specific projects."

A shrinking world means accessing talent that can reside anywhere on the planet. You don't need to hire that PhD who lives in China or India or central Africa—only engage her when a deliverable demands harnessing the global brain. Spouses working dual careers is the norm these days, demanding a more creative

---

[1] http://World Economic Forum, January 2016, The Future of Jobs www .slideshare.net/lrasquilha/world-economic-forum-report-future-of-jobs.

approach to work. People are living longer, which means a greater share of the workforce seeking the flexibility that will allow them to care for an ailing parent.

There have always been those intrepid souls hiring out their talents on a freelance basis. Think of the samurais in feudal Japan, whose skill sets were off the charts, or their modern-day equivalent, the mercenary soldier. Since the dawning of the computer age, prize programmers have been jobbing themselves out to the highest bidders in between ski vacations. All those graphic designers depicted in ads, working on the deck of their lakeside second home? They've been with us for decades as well.

Today we have the so-called digital nomad, enabled by technology. They meet with clients via Skype, collaborate with their coworkers inside a company using Google Docs. They may even be sitting next to you right now if you're reading this in a Starbucks. Venmo, Apple Pay, Google Wallet, and other mobile payment apps simplify online payments. JotNot Pro lets you scan your receipts, if not the next work agreement. Media accounts celebrate this "digital nomad" who needs nothing but a laptop, reliable Wi-Fi, and Skype to be in business. Yet it's been the rise of talent-access platforms that have truly liberated those who might otherwise be toiling away unhappily in a cubicle. The catch for any freelancer since the beginning of time has been one of matchmaking. Businesses need their talents. Freelancers want the work. But until recently, how did they find one another? Often the life of a freelancer has been feast or famine, steak or peanut butter—which drove many back into a corporate world they would have preferred to keep at arm's length.

To refrain and underscore the point: 89 percent of the workforce lacks passion for work. Sixty-seven percent feel overwhelmed. Is it any wonder that some are predicting that as many as 5 million people will join the freelancer ranks between 2015 and 2020? We're inclined to agree with Micha Kaufman, cofounder of Fiverr, who wrote in *Forbes*, "Now more and more of us are eschewing 9-to-5 jobs to plow our own paths, pursue our career passions, and wrest control of our daily grind. And that transformation is only accelerating. Soon, we'll look back on the desk-jockey era as a distant memory."[2]

* * *

We realize the vision we're laying out is not for everyone on the employee side of the equation. Some seek the predictability of the corporation. Not everyone is built to be a free agent, nor do they have the right skills to compete given the depth of talent at our site. An important distinction needs to be drawn between those who are freelancers by choice and those who have joined their ranks because of a lack of job opportunities.

Businesses that right-size themselves to run as leaner, more efficient entities that swell or shrink as needed will mean pain for some. It will mean layoffs and lost benefits and a lack of choice for some who would prefer full-time employment. Not everyone has an MBA from a top business school or a deep domain knowledge that they can successfully peddle on the open marketplace. We appreciate that Catalant is a platform for those on top of the talent pyramid. Others will feel threatened by the future that we're working to usher in. We appreciate, too, that there's a world of difference between the consultant able to work hard for a month or two, then surf or travel or spend more time with his kids—versus the driver working 50 or 60 hours a week to make ends meet.

Yet if the past couple of decades have taught us anything, it's that it's futile to fight technology. Change is inevitable. From our point of view, the right tactic is to embrace the new reality and do

---

[2]http://Micha Kaufman, December 2014, 2015, Forecast: You'll Never Work the Same Way Again, www.forbes.com/sites/michakaufman/2014/12/12/2015-forecast-youll-never-work-the-same-way-again/#5af0ca384bf.

what we can to advocate for those aspects of society that haven't caught up.

* * *

People are always asking us: If your platform is the future, why do we have full-time employees?

Part of the answer to the question is that every business needs them. What we're advocating is that leadership rethinks the way they engage knowledge workers and finds the optimal mix of permanent and independent people to run their business.

We've benefited tremendously from an internal version of our own business model: the use of external advisors in serious, part-time capacities. We've been able to attract incredible talent to work with us flexibly. In addition to Professor Fuller from HBS and Amy Villeneuve from Amazon, these ranks include Kylie Wright-Ford, former Chief Operating and Strategy Officer at World 50, a private global community of senior executives, and Bill Macaitis, former CMO of Slack and Zendesk, and SVP of Marketing at Salesforce. Brynn Thomas Harrington, Facebook's Director of People Growth, has been a key partner on human capital management, while Mark Roberge (former CRO at Hubspot) and Dave Walsh (former VP of Enterprise at Salesforce) played indelible roles in shaping our ultimate go-to-market organization. Vijay Subramanian, a critical player in building Rent the Runway, has worked with us for many years on building the correct systems to capture data most efficiently and accurately.

Like all businesses, we also need and want a corps of folks who are 100 percent devoted to growing our company. As Rob often reminds our company, having the years of audacious faith required to will a new market into existence requires almost irrational, complete devotion to the cause.

We know we're not there yet. We're still building out our system. We're proud of where we've gotten, but we'll be happier when we have 80 percent of the Fortune 1000, rather than

25 percent, regularly posting projects at our site. We sometimes need to pinch ourselves when we realize that 40,000 firms and experts have signed up with us. And securing an additional $41 million in financing, led by Highland and General Catalyst, in mid-2017, was an incredible accelerant for the future. But we're also looking forward to running an ecosystem with millions of participants, and work looks entirely different than it does today.

In some ways, however, the future is now. In 2016, a pair of prominent economists, Harvard's Lawrence Katz and Princeton's Alan Krueger, released a study of "alternative work arrangements" (temp workers, on-call workers, contract workers, freelancers). They found that their ranks jumped by 9.4 million between 2005 and 2015. Significantly, this was the entire net growth in employment during that period.

We're optimistic about the future. We feel excited by the potential of a dynamic new world where a lot more people are going to a have a healthier relationship with the workplace. More will enjoy their work, and businesses will have a powerful new tool for scoping out talent. Work will be done better by people who are happy to be doing it.

It's inevitable that this is our future. It's just a matter of time.

Index